Saber-Toothed Tigers: The History and Legacy of the Most Famous Extinct Cat Species

By Charles River Editors

Charles R. Knight's painting of a saber-toothed tiger

Introduction

A model restoration of a saber-toothed tiger

"Unrelenting angst through every fiber

Forever hanging over the precipice of defeat

It follows you: a rapacious saber-toothed tiger

Implacable stare, neither attacks nor retreats..." – Tom Quigley, *Savanna Mind* (2016)

It is difficult to ignore the effortless cool of a saber-toothed tiger. The fanged feline was equipped with the savage strength of a lion, the lethal stealth of a puma, the intimidating gait of a black bear, and the strapping, muscular arms of a gorilla. Amazingly, however, those traits did not stand out as much as the long, dagger-like fangs that earned the *Smilodon* its famous nickname. The saber-toothed tiger, legend has it, was as ferocious as it was fearless, often tackling beasts twice their size.

Saber-toothed tigers were arguably the most fabled of all the Ice Age creatures. The fearsome beast has earned itself quite the reputation, and it has been referenced to, appeared in, and inspired unique characters in endless books, films, comics, and other pop culture mediums. For example, Marvel's Victor Creed, otherwise known as "Sabretooth," is most known as Wolverine's nemesis, and he's depicted as a hulking, vigorously robust menace in a red and orange-gold jumpsuit with a hunched back, a shock of wild blond hair, tiger-like claws, and frightening fangs. As that indicates, the prehistoric creature is often portrayed as impossibly cunning, unfeeling villains. Even in films geared towards children, such as the first of the *Ice Age* animations, the saber-toothed tigers, excluding Diego, are depicted as vicious and vindictive, lawless fiends whose sights are set on a Neanderthal toddler.

The name and reputation of the ruthless saber-toothed tiger, as enduring as it is chilling, overshadows those of its contemporaries, and the fanged feline remains a household name and one of the foremost symbols of the Ice Age to this very day. So, what is it about the *Smilodon* that has captured – and continues to capture – the fears, morbid curiosities, hearts, minds, and imaginations of Holocene humans after all this time? And exactly how accurate is the general public's perception and understanding of the saber-toothed tiger? Moreover, if these saber-toothed beasts were indeed as merciless and indomitable as they are often portrayed, what was it that snuffed them out of existence? *Saber-Toothed Tigers: The History and Legacy of the Most Famous Extinct Cat Species* looks at the origins of the famous cats, the fossil finds, and theories regarding their extinction. Along with pictures depicting important people, places, and events, you will learn about saber-toothed tigers like never before.

The Dawn of the Fanged Feline

The Pleistocene Ice Age, unquestionably one of the most fascinating epochs in all of history, was so interesting that it seems almost removed from reality. For generations, kids have imagined the frost-laden ground quivering as a troop of woolly mammoths trudge across the rolling plain, their shaggy coats of fur and 13-foot-long, hook-like tusks glistening under the sun. Another posse of mighty woolly rhinoceroses follow in tow, with the foremost appendages of the double-horned, 6,000-pound beasts rising up to the heavens like the slender blade of a scimitar. Suddenly, an ominous chorus of heavy breathing rings in the air. Slicing through the fog are a sleuth of snarling, short-faced bears, their stunted facial features and their disproportionately lengthy – and muscly – arms and legs further enhancing the chill running down one's spine. This chill graduates to full-blown, paralytic fear when one sees the alpha prop itself up on its hind legs, towering over its counterparts at a height of 12 feet.

Robert Bruce Horsfall's depiction of a saber-toothed tiger fighting dire wolves over a Columbian mammoth carcass in the La Brea Tar Pits (1913)

Be that as it may, a glimmer of fear flashes in the eyes of even the mightiest of these beasts as soon as they hear heavy panting, followed by a guttural growl. These telltale sounds, often heard far too late, indicate the presence of an Ice Age beast like no other. Many of these animals, who know better than to spare another second, scampered off into the distance in all directions without so much as a second look, but those who failed to slip through the narrow slit that was the window of opportunity would be left to face the consequences. Judging by the ominous shadows that had suddenly unfurled across the snow, paired with the abrupt, hopelessly thick silence, even they likely understood that their prospects were bleak.

The calculated latecomers creeping in the shadows being described are none other than an ambush of saber-toothed tigers, otherwise known as the *Smilodon*, arguably the most renowned of all the prehistoric creatures that prowled around during this riveting period in time. Interestingly enough, this fanged feline was far from the largest of the Ice Age megafauna; in fact, they were medium-sized, about the equivalent of a modern-day lion, with even the largest species on average being about four feet tall at the shoulder and about seven feet long. While these dimensions are certainly nothing to scoff at, the saber-toothed tiger was easily dwarfed by any common mammoth and short-faced bear, and it competed for food with the likes of prehistoric lynxes, pumas, American cheetahs, and American lions (which are believed to have been 25% larger than modern lions).

In order to better understand the thrilling enigma that is the saber-toothed tiger, it would help to first clear up common misconceptions and assumptions that have been erroneously regarded as fact. To begin with, while the terms "saber-toothed tiger" and "saber-toothed cat" are often used interchangeably, they are actually two different things. To put it simply, not all saber-toothed cats were saber-toothed tigers, but all saber-toothed tigers were saber-toothed cats. At the same time, the saber-toothed tiger is the most well-known of all the saber-toothed cats. When people mention the saber-toothed tiger, they are actually referring to the *Smilodon*, a genus (the taxonomic category sandwiched between "family" and "species") derived from the machairodont subfamily of the *Felidae* (wild cat family) that stalked the Earth until about 10,000 years ago.

The confusion that continues to prevail is completely understandable. Disregarding pelt patterns and the seemingly negligible size differences between the different types of saber-toothed cats, the untrained eye struggles to tell these prehistoric felines apart. Saber-toothed tigers, like all other saber-toothed cats, had the low-slung proportions of a wild feline with similar small, flat ears, sinewy arms, powerful hind legs, and curved, "saber-shaped" canine teeth jutting out of either sides of their mouths, bared in full display, even when shut.

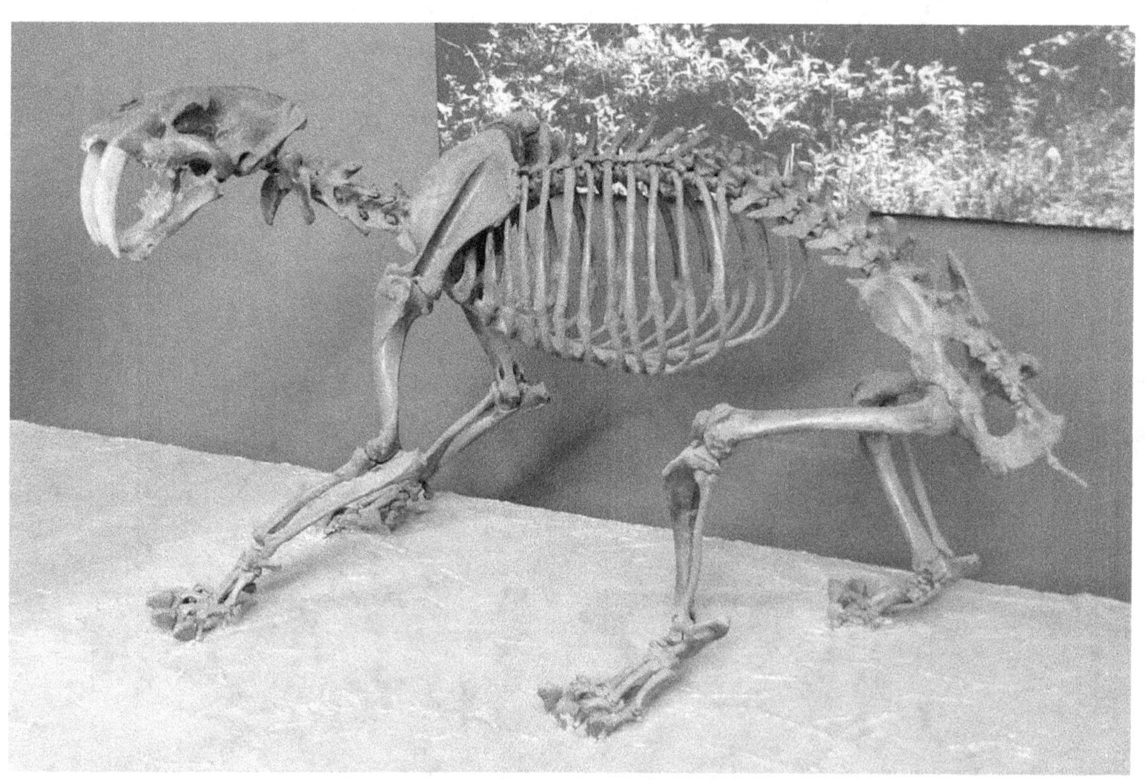

Ryan Somma's picture of a saber-toothed tiger skeleton

As marginal (and somewhat perplexing) as the differences among fanged cats might seem to lay people, they were nonetheless existent, with some of them being notable disparities. Under the extensive saber-toothed cat umbrella were a host of different *Feliformia* families, a suborder within the Carnivora order composed of carnivores with feline features, which included large and small cats, mongooses, civets, hyenas, etc. Such families included the *Nimravidae*, sometimes referred to as "false saber-toothed cats," which were distinguishable by their sharp, downward-projecting lower flange, which were the same length as their canines. They also included the

Barbourofelidae, a Miocene beast with a distinctive broader, mound-like protrusion on the back of its skull.

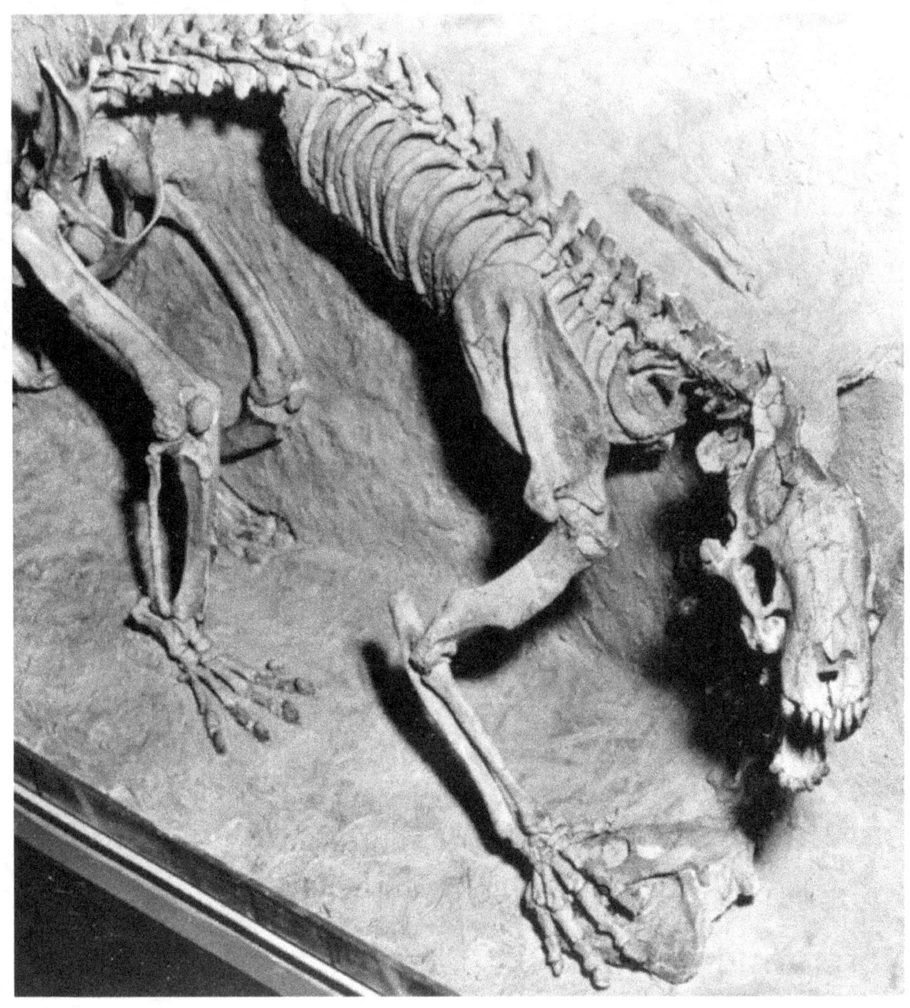

A *Nimravidae* skeleton

In addition to these families was the *Machaeroides* genus, the earliest known saber-toothed mammal, emerging in the Eocene Epoch (34-56 million years ago). It bore an even lengthier elongated skull and were on average no larger than a common dog. Its sister genus, the flat-headed *Apataelurus*, was equipped with larger canine teeth. Also incorporated into the saber-toothed cat family tree were two semi-marsupial lineages: the *Deltatheroideans,* a still-extant group of saber-toothed rodents of varying sizes, and the *Thylacosmilidae,* a now-extinct family of South American metatherian predators with almost comically large, clefted flanges that fit snugly between their canines and bent backwards at an awkward angle when their jaws were opened wide.

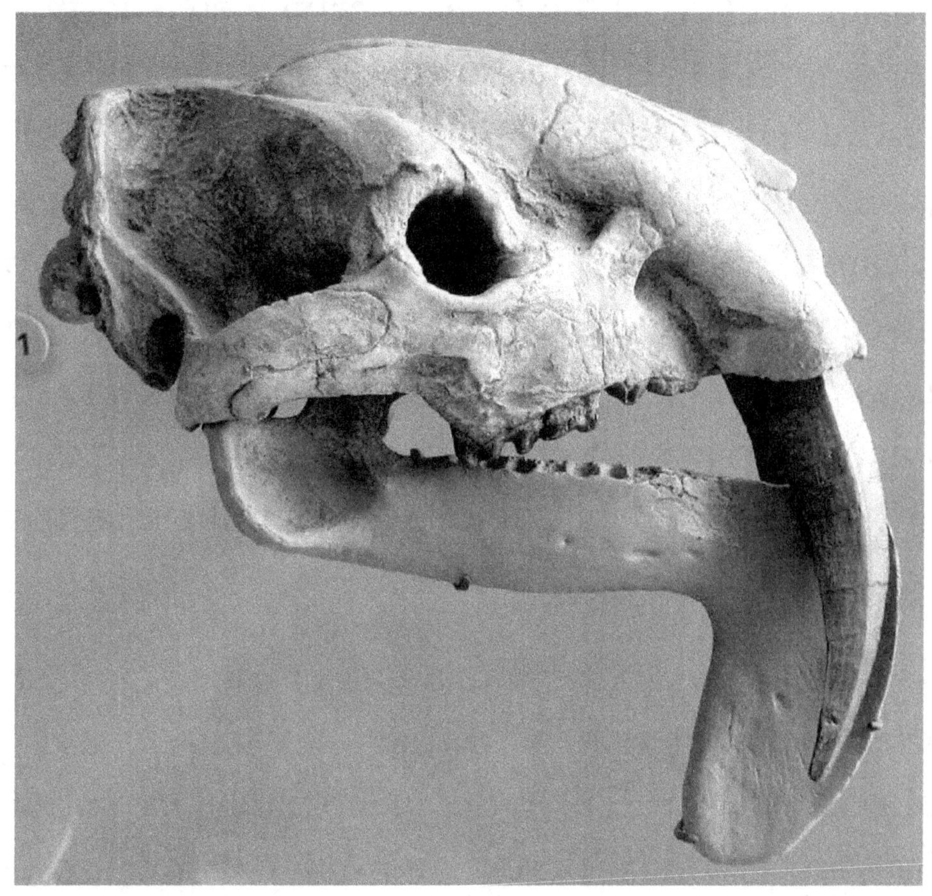

Claire Houck's picture of a *Thylacosmilidae* skull

The saber-toothed cat, categorized under the *Felidae* family, was generally a subfamily alternatively known as the *Machairodontinae.* The saber-toothed subfamily itself

was further split into three principal classes: the
Homotherini, also referred to as "scimitar-toothed cats";
the *Metailurini*, or "false saber-tooths"; and the
Smilodontini, or "dirk-toothed cats." The *Smilodon*, as its
name suggests, is under the *Smilodontini* tribe. These
felines, though closely related, were categorized
according to the differences in their prominent canines.
The coarse canines of the *Homotherini* were short,
slender, and more flattened in shape, with serrated tips.
Felines from the *Metailurini* tribe sported canines of
similar lengths, but these teeth were noticeably thicker in
width capped with smoother and duller tips, and therefore
less discernible in their protrusion. Descendants of the
Smilodontini tribe, on the other hand, had much longer,
often narrower, and observably sharper canines that often
extended well past their mandibles with finely serrated
tips.

   The saber-toothed tiger, like all other saber-toothed cats,
was the product of a phenomenon known as "convergent
evolution," which refers to the independent evolution of
similar traits among different, non-related creatures. One
example is the similar structure and functions shared by
the wings of bats, birds, and insects found across different
parts of the world. This is the antithesis of "divergent
evolution," a concept most popularly exemplified by
Darwin's finches, in which a single species branches out

and adapts to their new surroundings with the aid of different, freshly equipped evolutionary traits. The beaks of the finches scattered across the Galapagos Islands differed in shape and size, altered by necessity in accordance with the sources of food found in their habitats. The long, tapered canines of the *Smilodon* aside, those affected by the convergent evolutionary process also developed beefy limbs, husky torsos, and a yawning, cavernous gape. These evolutionary ingredients became so prevalent across various species that scientists often refer to the package as the "saber-tooth suite."

Another easily understandable, but still false assumption made about the saber-toothed tiger is its close kinship to modern tigers. Saber-toothed tigers are not at all closely related to tigers today, despite what the moniker indicates. In fact, saber-toothed tigers are not closely related to any living modern cat. This fallacious connection was first proposed in 1992 and upheld until 2005, when scientists contended that the *Smilodon* warranted its own separate lineage. This was confirmed in 2016.

No true descendants of the *Smilodon* or any other saber-toothed cat exist today, and only indirect offshoots that deviated from a mutual ancestor, long before the appearance of the *Smilodon*, have survived. This distant cousin in question is not a tiger, nor a lion, but the clouded leopard. Scientifically referred to as the *Neofelis nebulosa*, the long-lived carnivorous wild cat is equipped with dexterous, padded paws, short, but sharp canine teeth, and beautiful taupe-colored fur dappled with a distinctive pattern of dark stripes and blotches. It is primarily found in areas stretching from the Himalayan foothills to China, Indonesia, Thailand, and Borneo. Sadly, the clouded leopard is at risk of suffering the same fate, with their numbers dwindling as a result of illegal poaching and the crippling damage inflicted upon their natural habitats. The Formosan clouded leopard, once endemic to the island nation of Taiwan, is now completely extinct.

Cathleena Beams' picture of a clouded leopard

The clouded leopard is the only living mammal today with a cranial structure and cranium-to-canine ratio comparable to that of the saber-toothed tiger. On average, the upper canines of tigers, lions, jaguars, and other present-day felines measured less or no more than 20% of their skulls in length. The canines of clouded leopards, however, measured anywhere between 23-25% of their craniums in length. Of course, while indeed noticeably longer than that of their modern-day counterparts – considered an "outlier" by today's standards – the clouded leopard's statistics don't hold a candle to the saber-toothed tiger's cranium-to-canine ratio. The conspicuous canines of a typical *Smilodon* were at least half the length (or more) of their skulls.

Another parallel can be drawn between the jaw angles of the far-flung species. The clouded leopard discreetly possesses quite a few characteristics plucked from the classic "saber-tooth suite." Along with the clouded leopard's facial bones, which are rotated towards its hind end, much like other saber-toothed mammals, clouded leopards and saber-toothed tigers share an extraordinarily wide gape. According to the data published by Per Christiansen, author of a 2006 paper entitled "Saber-tooth Characters in the Clouded Leopard (*Neofelis nebulosa* Griffiths 1821)," the clouded leopard is capable of stretching its mouth open to a full 90 degrees, surpassing any other living wild cat or carnivore today. This trait, as Christiansen noted, is "a value normally considered feasible in extinct saber-tooths only."

A paper published by Rudemar Ernesto Blanco and his colleagues at Uruguay's Universidad de la Republica in the *Journal of Zoology* in 2013 has also linked the saber-toothed tiger to yet another unlikely, but probable distant relative. The astonishing identity of this distant relative is even more unexpected simply because it is not a wild feline, nor even a small, domesticated house cat, but a pint-sized marsupial known as the *Monodelphis dimidiata*, more commonly known as the "South American yellow-sided opossum." The connection lies in the length of the opossum's canines in proportion to the size of its body, which far transcends the ratios of any other living marsupial – both carnivorous and herbivorous – such as the Tasmanian devil and the Australian tiger quoll.

A sketch of the yellow-sided opossum in Charles Darwin's work

Examinations of the miniature carnivores' skulls, though only ranging anywhere between 45-100 grams in weight and roughly four to six inches in length, revealed upper canines that measured, on average, roughly three to seven millimeters, which jut out from both corners of their mouths, even when closed. Such canine-to-body proportions, Blanco and his colleagues insisted, was the hallmark of a saber-tooth predator, even exceeding the teeth-to-torso ratio of many extinct scimitar and false saber-toothed cats. The skull of a yellow-sided opossum also bore more resemblances to the cranial structure of a saber-toothed tiger, as opposed to the clouded leopard. This observation alone, Blanco concluded, knocked the clouded leopard off the top of the list of extant relatives to the saber-toothed tiger.

Bearing this in mind, the blend of saber-tooth qualities and "unspecialized traits" found in the yellow-sided opossum is believed to be the product of another evolutionary theory. Labeled "mosaic evolution," the concept revolves around traits emerging in a "patchwork" or "mosaic" pattern, which suggests that evolutionary processes are not always concurrent, but instead occur at a piecemeal pace. A 2013 article published by *The Evolution Institute* elaborated on this: "This means that some parts of a given species' skull could display characteristic saber-tooth features to a more extreme degree than others at a given point in time."

Other scientists have also identified traces of the saber-toothed tiger in the now-extinct saber-toothed salmon, as well as the extant saber-toothed walrus, the fanged musk deer, and warthogs. The flippered walrus is said to have the largest canines of all the extant saber-toothed creatures, with their teeth growing anywhere between 14-39 inches in length.

One of the oldest alleged ancestors of the saber-toothed tiger was the *Gorgonopsia*, which has been referred to as the "saber-toothed tiger of the Permian period." The *Gorgonopsia* were technically synapsids and tetrapods (four-legged creatures) that first emerged sometime during the Permian Period. This was the last period of the Paleozoic Epoch, which started during the final 47 million years of the Carbonifereous Period 298.9 million years ago to the early years of the Triassic period, which began some 251.902 million years ago. As synapsids, described as fossil reptiles that roamed the wild during the Permian and Triassic Periods, Gorgonopsians exhibited progressively mammalian traits to go with their reptilian qualities, and many of the Gorgonopsians (of which there were more than 30 genera) were the direct ancestors of full-fledged mammals.

  The Gorgonopsians, much like the saber-toothed tigers, were some of the most dominant predators in southern Africa, where they mainly resided; remnants of these ancient clade have also been recovered in Russia and China, as per the Pangea effect. Despite the reptilian nature of the various Gorgonopsian species, the creatures – particularly the largest in the clade – shared quite a few remarkable similarities with their supposed saber-toothed descendants. The largest Gorgonopsian, the *Inostrancevia,* ranged anywhere between the rhinoceros and the black bear in size and often feasted upon another clade of similarly-sized synapsids known as the "dinocephalians," as well as smaller, herbivorous para-reptiles called "pareiasaurs," a so-called "sister clade" to actual birds and reptiles. Like the saber-toothed tiger, Gorgonopsians were often dauntless apex predators that had no qualms about tackling beasts far larger than they were, with some dinocephalians measuring up to 15 feet in length and breaking the scale several times over at a weight of 4,400 pounds. The most salient of all these similarities, however, were the out-jutting canines of Gorgonopsian beasts, the most recognizable of all the saber-tooth traits, which allowed them to better gore and rip apart prey of all sizes. To put this in better perspective, the *Inostrancevia,* which reached up to 11.5 feet in length, paired with an average weight of 661 pounds, were equipped with sharp, saber-like six-inch canines – roughly a third of the length of their skulls.

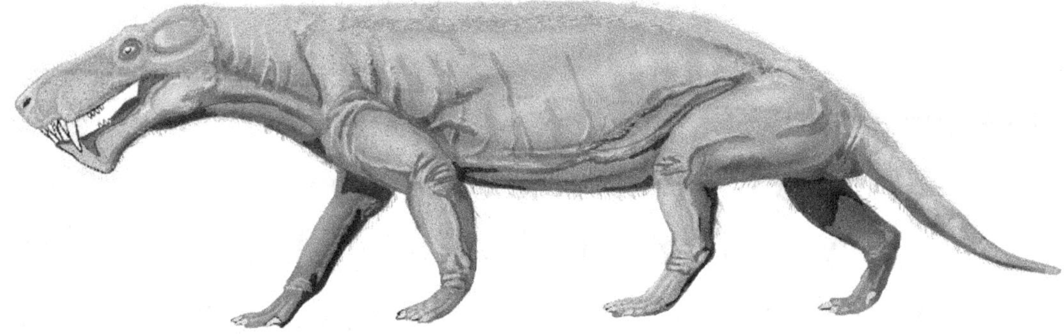

Dmitry Bogdanov's depiction of a *Gorgonops*

A number of research projects and studies conducted in the 21st century have also shined some light on the history of the *Smilodon* and even added new branches to the animal's family tree. In 2013, a new type of saber-toothed feline was unearthed in south-central Florida and named the *Rhizosmilodon fiteae* by paleontologists Richard Hulbert, Jr. and Steve Wallace. Up until that point, the only fossils that had been retrieved from these five million year-old pits belonged to those of two other saber-toothed cats: the *Megantereon*, a jaguar-like genus of the machairodontine saber-toothed cat that prowled the fields of Eurasia, Africa, and North America and bore flanges in its lower jaw that housed its prominent canines when its mouth was shut; and the relatively larger *Machairodus coloradensis*, which was endemic to North America during the late Miocene Period and bore long, thin, and flat canines on either side of its mouth. Upon examining the remnants of the *Rhizosmilodon fiteae,* which included a broken mandible and a chunk of the feline's cheek teeth, Hulbert and Wallace determined that the species belonged near the base of the bloodline wherein the *Megantereon* and the *Smilodon* diverged some 18 million years ago.

A model of the *Megantereon*

There are therefore two prevailing theories regarding the origins of the *Megantereon* and the *Smilodon*. The location of the *Rhizosmilodon* fossil, the oldest fossil of a saber-toothed feline found to date, indicates that both the *Megantereon* and the *Smilodon* may have first appeared in North America and later split from a common North American ancestor. From there, the *Megantereon* eventually wound up in and spread throughout Africa, Asia, and Europe, whereas the *Smilodon* stayed put in the Americas. The Blancan North American land mammal or faunal age, which began roughly 4.75 million years ago and wrapped up around 1.806 million years ago, also gave rise to two new species: the *Megantereon hesperus* and the *Smilodon gracilis*.

The second theory brings the similarities between the *Smilodon* and the *Rhizosmilodon* to focus. As maintained by some scientists, their similarities outweigh the similarities between the *Rhizosmilodon* and the *Megantereon*, which suggests the existence of an even more ancient and still undiscovered ancestor that fell between the *Megantereon* and *Smilodon* bloodlines that possibly dwelt in Africa or Eurasia. This would mean the ancestors from both lineages penetrated the North American realm at separate times. Either way, the unearthing of the *Rhizosmilodon* fossils in the five million year-old Floridian pits confirmed that the saber-toothed cats entered North America far earlier than previously believed.

Megantereon and *Rhizosmilodon* aside, the *Smilodon* also shared a mutual ancestor with the *Homotherini* (scimitar-toothed cats). Sometime in the 2000s, scientists endeavored in building "partial genome reconstructions" of a South American *Smilodon* specimen, alongside three different *Homotherini* specimen from North America and Europe. Thanks to the results of the meticulous experiment, a common ancestor to the *Smilodon* and *Homotherini* (also shared by all extant felines) was identified, and it is estimated to have existed approximately 20 million years ago. The uncanny genetic similarities between felines that resided on entirely different continents, as well as the marked gap in the saber-tooth fossil records in Eurasia, baffled many experts. Researchers also have yet to figure out a definitive reason for the appearance of *Homotherini* bones in Europe, which were found 200,000 years after they had been wiped out from the continent.

Rachel Lallensack, a contributor for the online magazine *Nature*, believed it was as simple and straightforward as the migration of prehistoric felines. She wrote, "The North Sea specimen could be evidence that the cats migrated back into Western Europe from Asia or over the Bering land bridge from North America." Offering another explanation for the seeming inconsistencies, she added, "Or it could be that the Eurasian *H. latidens* population dwindled to such low numbers that the animals just don't show up in the fossil record."

Johanna L.A. Paijmans of the German University of Potsdam, who spearheaded the partial genome reconstruction project, succinctly summed up the results of the experiment, as well as their fascinating implications: "Based on the mitochondrial DNA, we have estimated that house cats and saber-toothed cats shared a common ancestor about 20 million years ago...[This] is quite a deep divergence, considering that all modern cat-like species are estimated to have diverged 10-15 million years ago. House cats are thus closer related to tigers and pumas than to saber-toothed cats...This [also] means that a house cat is closer related to a [modern-day] tiger than the two saber-toothed cat species are to each other...”

These revelations in recent years have helped to further flesh out a better, albeit still hazy picture of the saber-toothed tiger's family tree, as well as the conditions that prevailed throughout the course of its complex evolution.

The earliest known felines first appeared during the Oligocene Epoch in Europe, which kicked off around 33.9 million years ago and ended roughly 23 million years ago. Although this relatively brief epoch lasted no more than 11 million years, a series of momentous changes – both evolutionary and climate-related – transpired. In addition to the alterations in the appearance and functions of modified appendages in numerous animals, as seen in primitive horses and elephants, a variety of new vegetation appeared. The new flora quite literally planted the seeds for the sprawling grasslands that cropped up during the Miocene Age that followed, and those grasslands served as sources of nourishment for the prey of the then-nascent *Smilodon*. Apex predators, including the *Smilodon*, were thus drawn to these sites, which were teeming with potential meals.

The migration patterns of saber-toothed felines and the *Smilodon* alike can also be attributed to other climate changes. The commencement and persistence of the Earth's cooling process, which lasted throughout the years of the Oligocene, played a rather critical role in shaping the habitats and behavior of various fauna. Underwater, marine creatures that could better endure colder temperatures migrated to areas further away from the heat of the equator, thus creating more biotic provinces. Mammals, on the other hand, began to proliferate on land, and with the exception of Australia, elephants, horses, camel, deer, primates, canines, and felines began to multiply across all continents. As these aforementioned mammals began to migrate from Asia to North America, and vice versa, the bloodlines of these mammals, including those of the saber-toothed tiger's ancestors, became further scattered. Much of the fanged feline's prey also began to swell in size thanks to their newfound access to flourishing savannas and grasslands.

Land bridges were key in the mass migration and diversification of land mammals throughout the Miocene. These routes were created by plunging sea levels and the petrification of inland seas, which then served as a bridge or a natural overpass between two continents that were previously inaccessible due to water barriers. One such water barrier was the Tethys Ocean, the Mesozoic body of water that separated Gondwana (consisting of Africa, South America, Arabia, India, Australia, Madagascar, and Antarctica) from Laurasia (Europe, Asia, and North America). Land bridges – primarily migratory avenues between Eurasia, North America, and Africa – allowed mammals such as the *Smilodon* access to new habitats, which they quickly adapted to due to the abundance of grasslands and prey.

The earliest known feline equipped with saber-tooth qualities was the *Pseudaelurus* genus, which first appeared in the Miocene, an epoch that began 23 million years ago and concluded roughly 5.3 million years ago. The *Pseudaelurus* species were the first to resemble present-day felines, with their sizes ranging from a house cat to a common lynx. These prehistoric felines had far lengthier spines, and traces of the extra molars they bore are still visible in the cheek teeth seen in saber-toothed cats and modern felines today. Brian Switek, author of the 2016 *PBS* article "The Making of the Cat," explained the significance of the *Pseudaelurus* in the development of the saber-toothed tiger: "This lynx-sized feline basically represents the standard cat body plan that would proliferate across the planet for the next 20 million years."

Felines during this time migrated to and from Asia to the Americas at least 10 times, which allowed for the evolution of numerous species and bloodlines across all continents other than Australia and Antarctica. In addition to the new breeds of horses that appeared in North America, such as the skinny, long-necked *Parahippus* and the donkey-like *Pliohippus*, which demonstrated the variegation of species that occurred during this period, the world acquired its first bears, canines, and hyenas, as well as the first saber-toothed cats belonging to the *Machairodontinae* subfamily. The alterations to the skulls and mandibles of these saber-toothed felines aside, their elongated canine teeth and increasingly wider gapes allowed them to tackle large animals with greater precision. The elongation of their canines came with the proportional lengthening and strengthening of their bodies; at the same time, the shortening of their lumbar regions and tails gave them more agility and allowed them to more effectively disable larger prey. Saber-toothed tigers, along with their other saber-toothed counterparts, were becoming fiercer and fiercer over time.

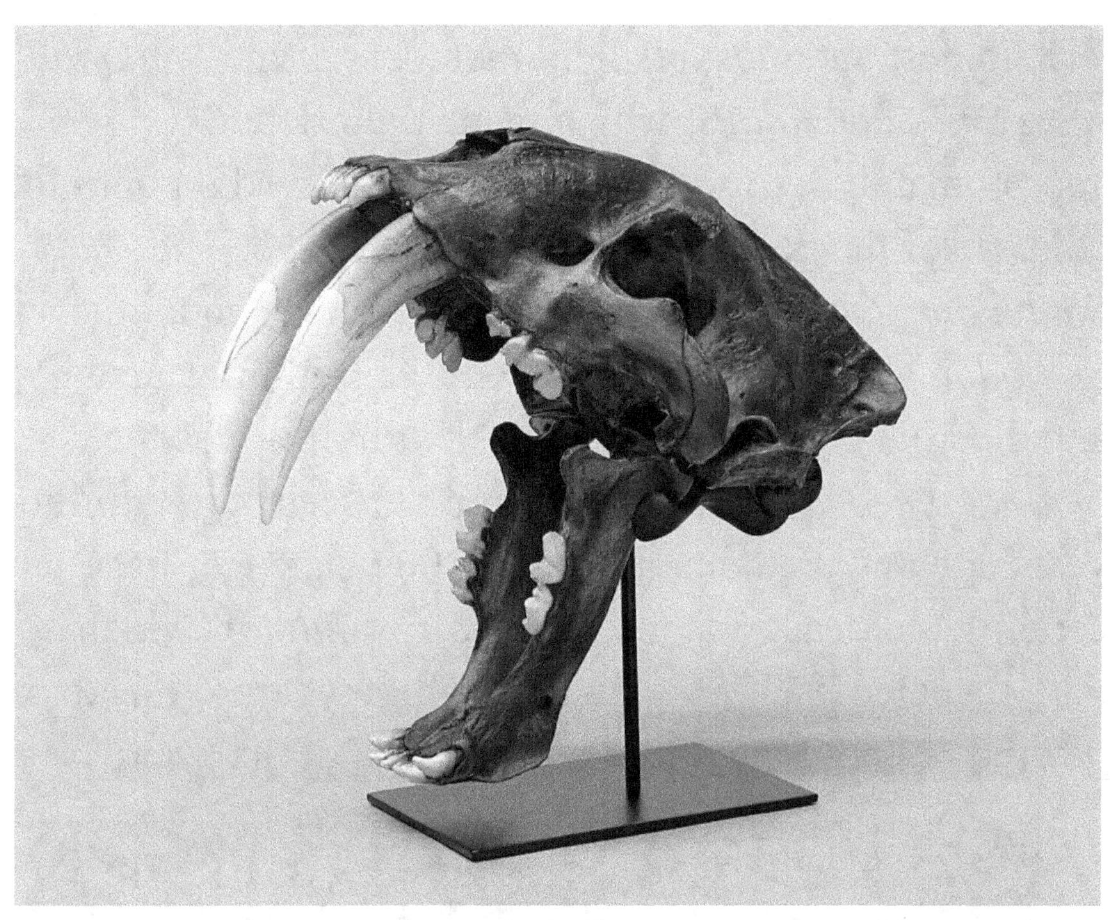

A picture of a *Smilodon fatalis* skull at maximum gape

The *Smilodon* emerged in North America and Europe during the Miocene and were dominating these regions by the time the Pliocene Epoch rolled around, which extended from 5.33 million years ago to 2.58 million years ago. It was during the Pliocene that the *Smilodon* migrated to Africa and Asia. The youngest breeds of these fanged felines continued onward to South America in the Pleistocene epoch that followed, which started 2.5 million years ago and rounded off about 10,000 years ago, otherwise known as the time of the most recent ice age.

The oldest and most resilient members of the *Smilodon* were *Smilodon fatalis,* which made their debut approximately six million years ago and lived on until the collapse of the genus about 10,000 years ago. The *Smilodon gracilis,* the second-oldest species under the *Smilodon* umbrella, first appeared five million years ago and died out 500,000 years ago. Next in line was the *Smilodon neogaeus*, which entered the scene three million years ago and died out about 500,000 years ago. Last, but certainly not least was the *Smilodon populator,* which only revealed itself roughly one million years ago and petered out not long after the extinction of the *fatalis.*

Michael B.H.'s picture of a *Smilodon populator* skull

Fernando da Rosa's picture of a *Smilodon populator* canine

As a whole, the *Smilodon* was far from the longest surviving species among prehistoric animals. The length of its existence, though nothing to sneer at, paled in comparison to cow sharks, which have existed for an estimated 175 million years, or crocodylians, which have been around for about 205 million years. Even so, the saber-toothed tiger more than made its mark in the history of the animal kingdom.

Tthe Mighty Machairodontinae

"A solitary saber-toothed tiger

Stalks her prey.

Her nails dig lightly into the scattered earth

Her eyes unwavering

Her coat flawless and her teeth pallid...

Looming above the jungle and the desert...” – Dan Miller, “The Saber-toothed Tiger”

Naturally, it’s impossible to comprehend the saber-toothed tiger's prowess without understanding its appearance and build in full detail. To put it bluntly, the fanged feline seemed to be a cross between a lioness and a cheetah on steroids, with a broad back and chest, thick, trunk-like neck, short, but muscular limbs, and its menacing, cutlass canines, often stained with the crimson of fresh blood. The average *Smilodon* was at least a foot shorter than a present-day lion, but it was close to twice the weight, and it rounded off its fearsome image with a bobtail. The stubby appendage was one of the many factors that differentiated the *Smilodon* from modern lions, leopards, and cheetahs, which are equipped with long, slender tails that provide them with the balance required for chasing down their prey. The compactness of the saber-toothed tiger's bobtail, as well as its long heel bones, which allowed it to leap with greater force, indicates that the *Smilodon* relied not on their speed, but the element of surprise when it came to eliminating their prey, underscoring its frightfulness twofold.

Innumerable illustrations and models of saber-toothed tigers have been circulating throughout the years, depictions based on a mix of fossil evidence, scientific theories, and artistic imagination. The skin and organic pelts of saber-toothed tigers, even those preserved in asphalt pits and permafrost, would have long decayed and dissolved, leaving nothing but bones behind. As such, scientists can only rely on educated guesswork to determine the color and patterns (if any) of their coats.

The felines of today possess coats that range from plain, solid colors and mesmerizing dark stripes to hypnotic spots. More often than not, the coats serve as camouflage and therefore correspond with the backdrops of their habitats. Felines who reside in open spaces brightly illuminated by natural light are more likely to don plain, yet glossy coats, whereas dwelling in dense, overgrown jungles and forested habitats, primarily preferring to stalk and hunt at nightfall, wear more glamorous coats streaked with spots and horizontal stripes. The same logic likely applied to the saber-toothed tiger. Saber-toothed tigers who frequented shrubby chaparrals and forested thickets would have been outfitted with striking constellations of stripes and spots, not unlike the *Dinofelis* (a genus of saber-toothed cats that belonged to the *Metailurini* tribe). Saber-toothed tigers, like other primitive felines who stalked the open country, would have had subdued, solid-colored coats (brown, tan, black, yellow-gold, and white) so as to better blend in with their backgrounds.

Subtle difference were also evident in the appearances of different *Smilodon* species. Broadly speaking, the *Smilodon populator*, which primarily thrived in South America during the Late Pleistocene (between 2 million to 10,000 years ago), was the most physically prodigious of all the saber-toothed tigers, weighing in at anywhere between 485-882 pounds and standing at about four feet in shoulder height. The length of an average *populator's* herculean torso, however, was more than twice its height, growing up to 8.5 feet in length, minus the tail. Naturally, the *populator,* as proportionate to the size of its body, was equipped with the longest of the saber-toothed tiger "bobtails," averaging around 11.8 inches in length. The *populator* had the largest canines, with medium-sized *populators* boasting thick, 12-inch fangs, 6.7 inches of which lay exposed with its mouth shut. The *populator* was also recognizable by its high-set, muscular shoulders, a prominent back that sloped downwards, and a slight hump between the nape of its neck and the slope of its back.

The *Smilodon fatalis* was a medium-sized feline, weighing anywhere between 353-617 pounds. The middling saber-toothed feline with seven-inch fangs was approximately 3.3 feet in shoulder height and about 5.7 to 6.6 feet in length sans tail, with a more level back in comparison to the *populator*. The *fatalis* appeared to be one of the most adventurous of the *Smilodon* species, as it could be found scattered across central and southern North America (including a large population in what is now Texas), the western part of South America, and Central America.

The *Smilodon gracilis,* also widely distributed across the American continents, was the most petite of all the *Smilodon,* weighing anywhere between 121-220 pounds, with smaller, sinewy proportions comparable to that of a modern-day mountain lion or cougar. The *gracilis* was nearly a whole foot shorter than the average *fatalis,* about 2.5 feet in shoulder height, and a torso measuring 6.5 feet lengthwise, bobtail included. Though the *gracilis* was typically smaller than a common *fatalis,* their canines were of similar lengths. Even so, while the fangs of the *fatalis* and the *gracilis* rarely exceeded seven inches, their bite forces were presumably more powerful than those of the *populator* since animals with shorter teeth are often able to deliver better controlled and more impressive bites.

Whether the saber-toothed tiger had the wherewithal to produce a rumbling roar is still a matter of debate, but most scientists believed they could. The voice boxes of felines are structured one of two ways. The first, which is composed of anywhere between 9-11 bones, allowed the feline to purr, but not roar. The second, which consists of five bones, two of which are tethered by an elastic ligament, allowed for the reverse. Considering the five bones found in the *Smilodon's* larynx, as well as the size and flexibility of the prehistoric feline's hyoid bone (otherwise known as "tongue bone"), it is reasonably safe to conclude that the saber-toothed tiger was equipped with the ability to roar.

Those hesitant to draw such a conclusion, such as Ashley Reynolds, an expert on fossilized felines from the University of Toronto, point to the larynges of snow leopards and other "pantherine cats." Though they are similarly structured and feature the same elastic ligament, these quiet felines do not roar. Reynolds explained, "It's not a direct one-to-one relationship between having that ligament and being able to roar, but it's certainly interesting to think that *Smilodon* may have had that ability."

The *Smilodon's* short, flat, and low-set ears, not unlike the big cats of today, further sharpened their hunting skills, as they could tune into a wide range of frequencies and an array of high-pitched noises, allowing them to discern different kinds of prey. The ear of a saber-toothed tiger would have been controlled by nearly three dozen muscles, which made possible a rotation span of 180 degrees. In comparison, the human ear is tooled only by three muscles and a trio of tiny, delicate bones.

Contrary to popular belief, it was not the canines, nor the teeth collectively, that made the saber-toothed tiger a force to be reckoned with, but rather its inordinately thickset and powerful front legs. The incredibly muscular legs of the *Smilodon* most likely compensated for the relative brittleness of its canines. As Julie Meachen, a vertebrate paleontologist and self-professed "Saber Cat Woman" of Des Moines University, put it, the *Smilodon* "must have used its forelimbs more than any other cats did." This makes sense because the canines of the saber-toothed tiger, not unlike present-day panthers and tigers, were far from invincible. Its bite force was packed with 220 pounds of crushing power, which exceeds the bite force of a human adult (161 pounds), but a modern-day lion, not equipped with oversized canines, has a bite force of 551 pounds. The *Smilodon's* canines were "circular in cross-section" and curved inwards, an evolutionary design that helped keep its canines and the rest of its teeth intact. If saber-toothed tigers simply sunk their long, slender canines into their thrashing, live prey, particularly those twice their size, in a bid to rip out of a chunk of their meat, they would not only fail miserably, but their canines would also most likely be severely fractured or snap off entirely. Instead, saber-toothed tigers knocked over their prey with their mighty forelimbs, which some say were powerful enough to tip over a full-grown bison, pinning it to the ground with its retractable claws and immobilizing them before going in for the kill. Meachen noted, "I found that they had very thick humerus cortical bones – much thicker than any non-saber-toothed cat living or extinct. I hypothesized that this extreme cortical thickening was correlated with the extremely long sabers. The robust limbs allowed *Smilodon* to restrain its prey so that it would be able to make a killing bite without damage to its saber teeth."

Of course, this isn't to say that their fangs were completely useless, as saber-toothed tigers used their fangs not as instruments for impalement, but as thin blades that sliced across the jugular and windpipes of their prey with almost surgical precision, which led to rapid blood loss, followed by occasional disembowelment and inevitable death. The *Smilodon's* jaws may not have been powerful enough to effectively strangle or crunch through the spines of their prey, but its fangs and teeth could tear apart the abdomens and other soft, fleshy parts of their kills, allowing them to consume even the largest of animals with ease.

Incidentally, it was the *Smilodon's* great gape, which measured an incredible 120 degrees, as opposed to the 60-degree gape of wild lions today, that kept the saber-tooth's teeth intact and allowed them the full and comfortable use of their complex teeth. Besides ripping apart large slabs of meat, canines were to a saber-toothed tiger what feathers are to a peacock. Simply put, it appeared that in the *Smilodon's* case, size mattered, as youthful, vigorous saber-toothed tigers with imposing, healthy canines were blessed with a higher chance of attracting mates.

That said, some scientists believe that the saber-toothed tiger's canines played a more vital role in the killing of their prey. According to them, the *Smilodon* may have used its exceptionally robust neck and sharp canines in tandem to paralyze and gore their kills, hurling its head back and forth and piercing the necks or any other exposed region of the creature repeatedly. This technique, however, has been ruled out by most other experts, as it seems too clunky and needlessly laborious to be regarded as a viable killing method.

Despite the somewhat disappointing vulnerability of *Smilodon* canines, the speed of their growth into an adolescent feline alone is proof enough that they were more than mere accessories. Saber-toothed tiger cubs, which, not unlike present-day felines, were born blind and feeble, were born with baby sabers. These baby sabers, like baby teeth, fell out and were quickly replaced by permanent adult sabers after a brief period of just 18-20 months. The canines of a juvenile modern-day lion grow, on average, about 0.1 inches, or three millimeters every month, whereas the canines of a developing *Smilodon* grew at close to three times that speed, extending by 0.3 inches, or eight millimeters each passing month. By the age of three, a *Smilodon* cub would have been equipped with fully developed seven-inch canines, which, for comparison's sake, is about as long as the space between an adult man's wrist to the tip of their middle finger.

Although the lifespan of an average *Smilodon* surpassed that of lions (which live between 10-14 years) and domesticated felines (which live an average of 15.1 years), the life expectancy of a common saber-toothed tiger, ranging from anywhere between 20-40 years, was still relatively short compared to some contemporaries. For example, the woolly mammoths averaged 70 years.

Whether their purely red-meat diets contributed to their abnormally long lifespans in the feline realm or the brevity of their life expectancy in the mammalian realm is another story. For the most part, saber-toothed tigers, when hunting solo, targeted visibly weaker and preferably wounded animals that were small to medium in size, such as deer, antelopes, and horses. Duos, trios, and full-scale packs, on the other hand, were far bolder and stalked larger, clumsier, more sluggish creatures like bison, oxen, hippopotamuses, mastodons, and mammoths. Based on the wear patterns on the teeth of several *Smilodon* fossils uncovered over the years, the fanged feline also consumed prong oxen, musk oxen, American camels, and ground sloths.

Some of the prey were exclusive to certain locations. The South American *Smilodon* preyed upon toxodonts (primitive hippo-like, elephant-sized creatures), litopterns (a prehistoric mammal that appeared to be a cross between a camel and an anteater), and other ungulates (hoofed mammals). In Florida, the *Smilodon gracilis* consumed the *Hemiauchenia* (an oversized prehistoric llama), *Glyptodonts* (armored ancestors of armadillos), and breeds of the boar-like *Platygonus* genus. Saber-toothed tigers would have most likely also been partial to human flesh.

Curiously, notwithstanding the saber-toothed tiger's understandably infamous reputation as a heinous, unfeeling, and bloodthirsty beast, some scientists believe its supposed viciousness is overblown, with researchers from one study going so far as to label it a "pussycat" in the world of wild felines. Researchers have referenced the lack of a perceptible size difference between male and female saber-toothed tigers as evidence of the saber-toothed tiger's semi-gentle nature. The following passage, from a 2009 article published by Duke University, explained, "In species where males fight for mates, bigger, heavier males have a better chance of winning fights, fending off their rivals and gaining access to females. After generations of male-male competition, the males of [certain] species evolve to be much larger than their mates." Wendy Binder of Los Angeles' Loyola Marymount University added, "Rather than [*Smilodon*] males having harems of females, the males and females in a group might have been more equal."

Given the lack of sexual dimorphism between both *Smilodon* genders, some scientists have proposed that packs of saber-toothed tigers were headed by an alpha female, not an alpha male, or an alpha pair may have shared the role. This is true for many present-day coyotes and wolves, which also share a consistency in the sizes of both genders. Moreover, like present-day wolves, families of saber-toothed tigers may have adhered to the "extended family" model. Aunts, uncles, and occasionally other elder relatives may have been tasked with looking after the children in the family den while the mother and father ventured out in the wild to snag supper for the family. Such an arrangement suggests that it took some effort and a rather prolonged length of time to look after saber-toothed tiger cubs. This theory is further shored up by the absence of juvenile *Smilodon* fossils at the La Brea Tar Pits.

Not only were female saber-toothed tigers supposedly deemed as equals, males were fairly territorial, but not overly aggressive when it came to seeking the attention of a potential mate, and this also contributed to the lack of a size difference between both genders. The *Smilodon* is also believed to have been a monogamous creature, taking on one mate and staying with them until one of them died.

Lingering Debates

As illustrations of saber-toothed tigers are most often seen amidst backdrops featuring icy cliffs, frost-covered trees, and endless, dense blankets of lace-white snow, or perhaps a humid, jungle-like thicket, the ground a jumbled mass of shrubbery, rocks, and trunk-sized roots, most have grown accustomed to associating the *Smilodon* with either of these contradictory habitats. The association is only logical, considering that the saber-toothed feline is thought to be an ambush predator, preferring to immerse themselves in the shadows of tree clusters or taking coverage behind icy boulders and outcrops when stalking their prey. In reality, the *Smilodon* was a versatile and adaptive animal, frequenting pine forests, jungles, wetlands, and temperate, highly wooded locales. The prehistoric felines were also inhabitants of dryer grasslands and plains.

The *Smilodon populator,* specifically, also acclimated itself to the "open, dry country" in South America, according to the results of a study conducted by Herve Bocherens of the University of Tubingen's Senckenberg

Center for Human Evolution and Palaeoenvironment. Bocherons had piloted a detailed perusal of a set of saber-toothed tiger bones dating back to 25000-10,000 BCE in the hopes of learning more about the *Smilodon's* dietary habits, which was then the largest feline breed on the continent. The carbon and nitrogen isotopes isolated from the specimen allowed Bocherons and his team to better understand the conditions of the South American *Smilodon's* habitat.

Prior to the publication of Bocherens' findings, it was generally believed that saber-toothed tiger strictly inhabited wet, wooded environments, which came with the promise of easy access to potable water sources such as swamps, marshes, rivers, lakes, and bogs; a colorful variety of plump, herbivorous prey; and plenty of opportunities for effective camouflage. The presence of *Smilodon* fossils in these South American areas, which provided only a fraction of the advantages listed above, stunned paleontologists around the globe who were now forced to take a second look at the *Smilodon's* hunting practices and other relevant behaviors. Naturally, the *Smilodon* that resided in these South American grasslands were presented with different sources of food, including the *Macrauchenia* (a steppe-dwelling, long-necked, and three-toed beast similar to litopterns) and two types of giant sloths: the *Lestodon* and the *Megatherium*.

Scientists today remain conflicted about the inherent nature of the saber-toothed tiger. On the one hand, there are experts who argue that the *Smilodon* was an ambush predator, and therefore a lone wolf, so to speak, not unlike leopards, cheetahs, tigers, and most other big cats, past or present. On the other hand, some claim that the saber-toothed tiger, like lions, hunted in prides, otherwise known as "collective hunting," and as such were social animals, ones who depended on their family and pack members for survival.

To begin with, the latter scientists pointed to the speed of the saber-toothed tiger's stride, which was encumbered by the uneven lengths between their forelegs and hind limbs. They were by no means slow animals, but it was highly unlikely that a solitary *Smilodon* would be fast enough to catch up with healthy and limber fast-footed animals like the deer. Furthermore, these scientists referenced the abundance of severe fractures, debilitating injuries, and degenerative diseases found in *Smilodon* bones over the years. The likelihood of overcoming such wounds and ailments alone, which came with not only agonizing physical pain, but also the compromising of the animal's ability to hunt for prey or defend itself effectively, would be bleak at best. At the same time, most of that specimen displayed signs of healing and regrowth, which would have taken extensive periods of time. That could only have been accomplished with the aid of family or pack members. This suggested that able-bodied saber-toothed tigers most likely shared their kills with the wounded members of their prides and possibly even nursed them back to health.

Christopher Shaw, a paleontologist and former employee of the La Brea Tar Pits and Museum, made note of a pelvis that was heavily disfigured by an unknown external force after it was discovered at the famous asphalt seeps: "There was a lot of infection, pain, and smelly stuff, and just a really awful situation for this animal, but it survived well over a year. To me, that indicates [the wounded *Smilodon*] was part of a group that helped it survive by letting it feed at kills and protecting it."

As a result, it seems the hunting strategies of the *Smilodon* would have differed based on the habitat and different kinds of species. Smaller and therefore physically lighter saber-toothed tigers, such as the *gracilis*, might have perched itself on a tree canopy before pouncing upon some hapless creature passing by. It could then wrestle its prey to the ground and complete its kill by slicing open its jugular or some other exposed and vulnerable part. Conversely, the size and weight of the *populator* would have impeded its ability to lurk from great heights. Although the feline may have easily prepped for its ambush from atop a great boulder instead, scientists believe that they would not have solely relied on this particular kill method, as it was deemed too "passive." A beast of the *populator's* size would have required both larger prey, and a more regular feeding schedule. As such, scientists concluded that the larger *Smilodon* would have opted to hunt with company, which heightened their chances of effectively capturing and slaying larger, more filling prey.

Some scientists wondered whether the *Smilodon* even employed the "drop and kill" tactic at all. Judging by the dime-sized dimensions and the placement of the sabered-tooth tiger's eyes, the feline would have had below-average eyesight and thus lacked the razor-sharp depth perception possessed by leopards and other tree-lurking cats. The *Smilodon's* thickset build and the awkward proportions of its limbs would have also made climbing trees and great heights a chore.

As much as the *Smilodon* may have valued close-knit relationships and its supposedly passive "pussycat" nature, at the end of the day, saber-toothed tigers were wild animals, meaning that infighting was still very much existent. A paleontologist from Buenos Aires' Bernardino Rivadavia Natural Sciences Argentine Museum, Nicolas Chimento, who authored a study that inspected the injuries found in the skull of a *Smilodon,* noted, "Although it cannot be ruled out that the injuries were caused by a potential prey kicking the skull, the size, shape, and general features of the injuries suggest that they were inflicted by the upper canines of another *Smilodon* individual during agonistic interactions." The gash, Chimento concluded, may have been the product of a territorial tussle, or perhaps a skirmish over prey.

The large number of *Smilodon* fossils found at or near the La Brea Tar Pits and other such traps of nature reveals yet another interesting aspect about the hunting habits of the saber-toothed tiger. Saber-toothed tigers who mistook mammoths and hefty ungulates misleadingly ensnared in the sticky pools of charcoal-black asphalt as free, tasty feasts served to them on silver platters often became entangled in the death traps themselves, eventually resulting in their own slow and torturous demise. This indicated that the *Smilodon* also exhibited scavenging tendencies when the opportunity presented itself. For the most part, however, *Smilodon* were chiefly active predators, a quality instilled in all felines across the board.

Charles R. Knight's painting of a *Smilodon fatalis* approaching a trapped *Paramylodon* at the La Brea Tar Pits

Furthermore, the presence of saber-toothed tiger fossils in tar pits provided more proof that supports the *Smilodon* pride theory. The *Smilodon* whose gruesome fates were sealed by the tar pits had most likely been lured by the howls of the animals trapped in the sludge. According to researchers who studied the reactions of African carnivores to the distress cries of various prey, predators that hunted in packs were most likely to respond, as one would to the ringing of a dinner bell. Solitary hunters, conversely, tended to steer clear of such sounds, as they knew that they would be outnumbered by the pack of competing predators it was bound to attract.

Given its position at the top of the food chain, the *Smilodon* had no natural predators. Still, saber-toothed tigers had to compete with quite a few other carnivores, such as the *Panthera leo atrox* (the American lion) and the dire wolf, for sustenance. One can imagine the carnage that ensued amongst these carnivorous beasts whenever food was scarce.

A picture of mounted skeletons of a *Smilodon fatalis* and a dire wolf

The *Smilodon's* hunting opponents may not have only been restricted to other four-legged carnivores. Although there is little concrete evidence to support it, scientists believe that the saber-toothed tiger most likely crossed paths with early humans at least occasionally, if not on a regular basis. The *Smilodon* themselves may have also been targeted by prehistoric human hunters for food and other purposes – and vice versa – but the majority of saber-toothed tigers who perished at the hands of people were most probably killed in self-defense.

Two perforations situated on the skull of a hominid dating back 1.75 million years and discovered in the Republic of Georgia were determined to be perfectly compatible with the distinctive canines of a species belonging to either the *Homotherini* or *Smilodontini* tribe. The locations of these perforations (one on the back and the other on the bottom of the cranium) suggests that the hominid victim had been facing upwards when he was pinned to the ground. The feline then wrapped its jaw around the crown of its victim's head and later sank its canines into the spinal cord of its prey.

A separate trove of fossils unearthed in a former coal mine in Schoningen in October 2015, which yielded five 300,000-year-old *Smilodon* teeth and a shard of arm bone belonging to a separate feline, was found at a site that previously produced fragments of ancient human spears. This, the researchers behind the dig believe, was proof that the saber-toothed tiger and *Homo heidelbergensis* (a subspecies of archaic humans) coexisted in Europe. The humerus, the scientists added, appeared to have been chiseled into the shape of a primitive hammer, which led them to conclude that some saber-toothed cats were hunted, if not for food, then for their bones and other remnants, which were fashioned into tools by early humans.

A recent discovery of a nearly intact *Smilodon* posterior skull with basal crania, recovered by a diver in a sinkhole in Marion County, Florida, also hints at what may have been an encounter between a saber-toothed tiger and an early human. The skull, which belonged to a 20,000-year-old *Smilodon fatalis,* was discovered near what appeared to be a spearhead fragment made of either bone or stone, supposedly of Pre-Clovis origin (a term used to describe Native American tribes that existed some 50,000 years ago). More importantly, there appeared to be a diamond-shaped hole, no more than 1.2 inches in width, on top of the skull's right temporal bone, which closely resembled the impression left behind by such spear projectiles.

If the saber-toothed tiger had indeed become a common target of prehistoric human hunters, they would not have been killed by bows or arrows, but by spears and projectiles (Clovis points and atlatls) carved out of stone, animal bones, or mammoth tusks. Later generations may have elected to use war clubs (stone bludgeons with blunt, rounded heads and occasionally spikes), axes, and other early tomahawk-like instruments. Human hunters may have also relied on less aggressive, or less confrontational hunting tactics. For example, they may have acted as bait and sent them hurtling off cliffs, later gathering their carcasses below. Some speculate that early humans constructed pits laden with spikes and other booby traps similar to those they built for mammoths, or bound potential *Smilodon* prey to trees to lure the fanged carnivores, which they then ambushed. Early humans may have also enlisted the aid of domesticated dogs that could track down saber-toothed tiger dens, where they could then descend upon *Smilodon* kittens and younglings.

The Extinction and Rediscovery of the Saber-Toothed Tigers

"It is evident that one cannot say anything demonstrable about the problem before having resolved these preliminary questions, and yet we hardly possess the necessary information to solve some of them..." – attributed to Georges Cuvier

Since the concept of written records has only been around for about 5,000 years, no firsthand accounts of the saber-toothed tiger exist. Owing to this absence of pertinent information, all descriptions of the fanged feline were made thousands of years after they went extinct, based upon anatomical deductions and educated guesses. Likewise, as there are no authentic records of last *Smilodon* sightings to reference, it is impossible to accurately establish the year of extinction. Scientists must instead rely on a slew of other clues, taking into account regional history, environmental factors, and more, to piece the puzzle together.

The general consensus within the scientific community today is that the *Smilodon* was flushed out of existence about 10,000 years ago as a result of a phenomenon now referred to as the "Quaternary extinction event." This estimate was partly derived from the ages of the youngest *Smilodon* fossils that have since been exhumed across the Americas. The latest North American specimen to be discovered, belonging to a *Smilodon fatalis*, was found in Pit 67 of the La Brea Tar Pits in 2012 and was said to be approximately 13,025 years in age. The youngest *Smilodon* ever found in South America, a *Smilodon populator* uncovered in the Cueva del Medio cave in Chile's Magallanes Region in 2010, was approximately 10,935-11,209 years old.

An even younger *Smilodon* was supposedly unearthed in 1973, as documented by numerous publications, including a *Time* magazine article entitled "Tiger in the Bank." In the early hours of August 6, a crew of construction workers finished off the last of their coffee, rolled up their sleeves, and prepared to erect the foundations of what was soon to be a 28-story branch of the First National Bank in Nashville, Tennessee. The laborers proceeded to level out four old Native American mounds and cleared out 30 feet of limestone and earth with the aid of scrupulously placed sticks of dynamite and heavy-duty drilling equipment. Work suddenly screeched to a halt, however, when an eagle-eyed construction worker fished out from the earth an "ivory-colored, banana-shaped object that looked like a miniature elephant tusk." Upon closer examination, the strange object was revealed to be nothing other than the canine of a saber-toothed tiger. The fang was estimated to be roughly 9,410 years old, which indicates that the *Smilodon* may have clung on to survival for some time longer. That being said, 21st century scientists take this conclusion with a grain of salt, as they have little faith in the precision of outdated 1970s carbon dating technology.

Like any other extinct genus, particularly from the Pleistocene Epoch, the reason or reasons for the *Smilodon's* extinction continue to be a matter of contention. The fact that such a strikingly dominant and resilient beast was even wiped out of existence in the first place is a sobering pill that many find difficult to swallow.

Unlike the dodo bird, which could only lay one egg at a time (a fact that possibly contributed to their fast-shrinking numbers during their final years), saber-toothed tigresses produced an average of three cubs per litter following eight-month-long gestation periods, which in turn suggests that the *Smilodon* maintained healthy and fairly large populations during their prime. What's more, saber-toothed tigresses, along with all other mothers found across nature, feline and otherwise, would have been very protective of their young. Given their substantial builds, intimidating canines, and retractable claws, among other saber-tooth defense features, the fanged tigresses would have been more effective than just about any other animal in fending off unwanted company. In other words, this genus of prehistoric felines seemed almost unconquerable, so what was it that signed their death sentence?

  Some theories point to the dramatic climate change that ensued during the Quaternary Period. Around the world, glaciers began to recede, sheets of ice drifted and disintegrated, and chunks of ice rained from the thawing cliffs above. A drastic seasonal shift, which came with changes in precipitation rates, remodeled the conditions of various ecosystems across the continents. In a short spell of just 5,000 years, temperatures spiked more than six degrees. These momentous changes consequently triggered the Quaternary Extinction Event towards the final years of the last Ice Age, which saw a startlingly wide variety of megafauna vanish from the face of the Earth en masse. In less than 1,500 years, 15 kinds of megafauna weighing over 220 pounds were stamped out in North America alone, with 74% of all animals (45 of 61 genera) on the continent disappearing in total. South America lost approximately 82% (58 of 71 genera) of this kind of wildlife. One can compare this to the total number of faunal species that have been rendered extinct in the last 50,000 years, which scientists believe is under 35.

While some scientists think the marked spike in temperatures spelled the demise of the saber-toothed felines, others assert that the *Smilodon* would have been able to withstand the rising temperatures since it had survived other dramatic climate changes in the past. The bobtail, small, flat ears, and coat of short, but coarse and bristly fur assigned to the *Smilodon* by evolution, they say, would have allowed the prehistoric feline to keep warm in frigid temperatures and keep cool in more tropical areas at the same time. The fanged felines most likely suffered discomfort amidst the heat waves rippling across their terrains, but they would have adjusted.

Nevertheless, the saber-toothed tiger may have still very well been affected by indirect, yet fast-acting and irreversible consequences generated by these seasonal changes. Although one could claim that the saber-toothed tiger was merely inconvenienced, but not daunted by the increasingly persistent heat, one could not say the same about many herbivorous megafauna, the *Smilodon's* usual prey, as they dropped like flies in the figurative blink of an eye. The diminishing populations of these megafauna, some scientists believe, left the *Smilodon* with no choice but to stalk smaller animals instead. Their inability to keep up with these smaller-boned, and therefore exceptionally agile animals, may have led to undernourishment and mass starvation, and even when they succeeded in scoring an opossum or some other nimble-footed creature of some kind, they were made to share what little meat their catch offered amongst themselves. A saber-toothed tiger, which required considerably more flesh than the average feline to fuel their sizable bodies, could consume up to 66 pounds of meat in one sitting.

Competition from other carnivores in their ecosystems, which undoubtedly intensified, may have also contributed to the starvation of the saber-toothed tigers. At one point, Californian scientists posited that the saber-toothed residents of La Brea were subjected to a notable period of starvation in their final years, primarily citing dental evidence gathered from a number of *Smilodon* specimens. The shortage of prey in the area, they say, prompted local saber-toothed tigers to resort to consuming the entire carcasses of their kills – bones and all – as indicated by the disfigured canines, chipped in various ways, that had been extracted from the pits.

As fascinating as the theory may be, Larisa DeSantis, a vertebrate paleontologist at Nashville's Vanderbilt University, is one of a few who have since sought to lay this theory to rest. Instead, DeSantis insists that the dental microwears were the products of close-combat struggles with prey and other beasts, and that they were not consistent with patterns usually left behind by bone-gnashing. On a related note, some of the experts who side with DeSantis have chosen to scrutinize this theory from another angle, because they think the *Smilodon* was never starving at all.

Inevitably, humans have also been blamed for the extinction of the saber-toothed tiger. Early tribesmen contended with the fanged felines for natural resources and what was left of the herbivorous prey, which, besides climate change, further threatened the *Smilodon's* plummeting food supply. Others wondered if the feline had been hunted into extinction at the hands of early humans, with their pelt, bones, and other remnants possibly used for food, shelter, and the construction of tools or musical instruments. If the tribesmen found little to no use with a saber-toothed carcass, perhaps the prehistoric felines had been slaughtered as a safety precaution by those who had no understanding of the dangers of overhunting.

According to other scientists, particularly those in California, while humans were certainly key (albeit oblivious) contributors to the genus' undoing, their lasting impact may have been more indirect, and even outwardly subtle. The proliferation of the human population, for instance, brought about their invasion of more *Smilodon* habitats and would have accelerated the shrinkage of the feline's already-dwindling population. Some have also theorized that early tribesmen who had migrated to the Americas from other parts of the world brought with them an array of highly infectious foreign diseases and lethal viruses, and that they may have spread to a wide range of mammals, including the saber-toothed tiger.

A 2014 study published in the *Quaternary International* journal, in addition to a separate study published two years later, confirmed that humans – no matter to what extent – were among the culprits behind the *Smilodon's* extinction. The study, fronted by Chris Sandom of the *Wild Buisness, Ltd.* firm and his team, aimed to prove that the "loss of species correlates more closely with the arrival of humans than with changes in climate." Under Sandom's instructions, researchers compiled a list of 177 different species that had vanished completely between

132,000 and 1,000 years ago. From the results, the researchers concluded that sub-Saharan Africa and Eurasia were home to the lowest number of species-wide extinctions. The majority of these extinctions, instead, occurred in the Americas, as well as Australia, which played host to significantly higher human populations. Stephanie Pappas of *Live Science* broke down the findings, writing, "Overall, the results demonstrated that [mankind's] arrival was responsible for 64 percent of the variation in extinction rates around the globe, while temperature changes explained 20 percent of the variation, mostly in Eurasia."

Following the *Smilodon's* extinction, the fanged feline remained entirely forgotten, buried deep within the sands of time and on the fringes of human memory, until it emerged for the first time in modern history in the early 19th century. In the mid-1830s, a daring and prolific Danish naturalist named Peter Wilhelm Lund, accompanied by an assortment of assistants, headed down to the calcareous (rich in calcium carbonate) caves by the town of Lagoa Santa in Minas Gerais, Brazil. These caves had recently become a popular mining site, singled out by entrepreneurs looking to cash in on the saltpeter founts, a white, chalky powder used for agricultural and medicinal purposes. It was also an ingredient used in the recipe for gunpowder.

Lund

Lund was appalled by the constant and careless mining of these caves, for workers were inadvertently causing the destruction of priceless and irreplaceable fossils, so he and his team hastened over to these caves at once to retrieve as many of what was left of the untouched fossils as they could. It didn't take long for Lund to thank his lucky stars for having followed through with his decision, because it was here that he made his career and history-defining discovery: a stratum, which he referred to as a "glacial drift," brimming with Pleistocene faunal fossils, such as the *Eremotherium laurillardi,* otherwise known as the "Panamerican Ground Sloth," and the *Protopithecus brasiliensis*, the largest "New World Monkey" that ever existed. More exciting yet, Lund spotted a number of fragments belonging to an unrecognizable prehistoric feline, one that appeared to have been equipped with impressive tusk-like canines.

On paper, Lund, often referred to as the "father of Brazilian paleontology," seems to have been perfectly cast for the discovery. By the time the Danish-Brazilian zoologist, paleontologist, and archaeologist stumbled upon the saber-toothed tiger in 1835, he had already earned himself a glittering reputation within the European scientific community and beyond, which had been enhanced by the two prize-winning dissertations he authored. Moreover, shortly after receiving his doctoral diploma from the University of Kiel just six years prior, Lund relocated to Paris, where he forged a solid friendship with Georges Cuvier. Cuvier, then the resident professor of comparative anatomy at the Parisian Museum of Natural History and the foremost naturalist of the era, was praised for his pivotal and ground-breaking ideas. It was Cuvier who first popularized the notion of mass extinction, as well as the theory of "catastrophism."

Cuvier

Strangely, little else is known about the details surrounding the discovery of the fanged feline apart from the presence of four other characters: the Danish botanist Eugen Warming, most famed for composing the first-ever book on plant ecology; a Norwegian artist and cartographer, Peter Andreas Brandt, employed as an illustrator; and most importantly, unsung heroes in the form of a pair of unnamed slaves, who performed all the actual physical labor.

Initially, in 1839, Lund intended to call the new genus *Hyaenodon*, and the species he discovered, the *Hyaena neogaea,* as the source of the isolated bones retrieved from the caves was misidentified as a hyena. Lund continued to operate under this erroneous assumption until he was presented with a few more molars and foot bones belonging to the same mysterious beast. Three years later, it finally dawned on Lund that the specimen was no hyena, but rather, a separate species found in the family of felids; it was then, in 1842, that Lund first coined the term *Smilodon,* a play on, or blend of two Ancient Greek words: *smilē,* which translates to "double-edged knife," or "scalpel," and *odontús,* meaning "tooth." The *Smilodon* species that he had discovered was from thenceforth to be known as the *Smilodon populator,* the latter term meaning "destroyer," or "one who brings devastation."

Not long after this revelation, Lund became the first to publish a written description of the saber-toothed tiger. He wrote in part, "Regarding its size, this unique extinct carnivore rivaled the largest known cats or beras; the size of its canines is very much larger than in any species of carnivore, living or fossil. Judging by the dimensions of its foot bones, its body must have been heavier than that of any of the living felines...It is evident that a carnivore of such size with such formidable weapons must have reaped abundant victims...[in the] ancient world. In fact, I found the remains of its prey in three different caverns, which included...great accumulations of bones of diverse animals, many of them gigantic in size..."

In 1868, a second species of *Smilodon* was isolated and identified by Philadelphian paleontologist and father of the Neo-Lamarckism school of thought, Edward Drinker Cope. This new species, however, was christened by another Philadelphian paleontologist and anatomical expert, Joseph Leidy, who proceeded to name the breed the *Smilodon fatalis.* The etymology behind the word *fatalis,* is unclear. The word was a direct reference to the Latin term *fatalis*, some say, which translates to "destiny" or "fate." Others say it was derived from the English word fatal, a synonym for "lethal" or "death-dealing." The *Smilodon fatalis* was not the topmost item on his list of names. Above it were the terms *Felicis (Trucifelis) fatalis,* (the first name for the North American Smilodon), and the *Trucifelis fatalis,* for short, which were eventually struck off.

The *Smilodon gracilis* received its name from Cope in 1880. How exactly Cope landed upon the name is unknown, but most believe it to be inspired by the lighter, more "graceful" build of the species. It was also Cope who first recognized the *gracilis* as a separate species in its own right after examining an upper saber-feline canine root, which was noticeably smaller than the average *Smilodon* fang, paired with a "more compressed base that had been recovered from Pennsylvania's Port Kennedy Cave. The names for other *Smilodon* species identified in the years that followed, such as the *Smilodon floridanus* (also named by Leidy in 1889) and the *Smilodon californicus* (named by an O. Bovard in 1907), were less imaginative.

The advancements in modern science's understanding of the saber-toothed tiger were in large part propelled by the extensive and still-ongoing excavation projects at the Rancho La Brea Tar Pits in Los Angeles. The most popular premise is that the tar pits' origins date back 5-25 million years, when the land that would one day become Los Angeles lay submerged underwater in a shallow expanse that hosted single-celled organisms similar to marine plankton. When these single-celled organisms eventually shriveled up and wasted away, they sank to the seabed, cumulatively transforming into a dense blanket of sediment.

Due to climate change, continents and bodies of land continued to shift as the watery expanse slowly evaporated. The remnants of the deceased plankton, after their once-watery graves were trapped under tons of sediment, gradually recast themselves as oil and gas deposits. The crater was slowly refilled by rainwater and the thaw of the Ice Age, and sediment continued to stack up in tandem with the spinning hands of time. The crushing weight of the increasing sediment, coupled with the immense mass of the ocean, heated up the sheets of carbon-filled organic matter. Owing to the absence of oxygen, the compressed matter then converted to fossil fuels, namely crude oil, or petroleum.

The actual formation of the La Brea Tar Pits occurred about 35,000-40,000 years ago, once the sea had ebbed. Heated founts of petroleum and crude oil miles upon miles underneath the surface bubbled up through the cracks between the splintered rocks above the Salt Lake Oil Field, resulting from periodical earthquakes stemming from the movement of tectonic plates in the Los Angeles Basin, which served as unrestricted pathways to the surface. The coat of petroleum that had traveled up to the surface eventually evaporated, which left behind puddles of rich, syrup-like asphalt, otherwise known as pitch.

An early 20ᵗʰ century picture of the tar pits with oil derricks in the background

The quiet deceptiveness of the inescapable sludge was rounded out by its misleading ability to sustain the growth of flora. The trees and foliage that sprung forth here were enough to seduce the unsuspecting creatures into taking a gander; the leaves and twigs shed by the surrounding flora were the garnishes to these coal-black stews. After about an average of 17-20 weeks, the rigid corpses of the hapless animals that found themselves trapped in the pits vanished underneath the tar's bubbly surface. The pelts and shells of these creatures melted away, but their bones, on the other hand, remained intact, almost expertly preserved by the contents of these sticky time capsules.

In 1828, a 4,439-acre (roughly seven square miles) strip of land encompassing the tar pits was designated the title of "Rancho La Brea" via a Mexican land grant, and it was entrusted in the care of a pair of business partners named Antonio Jose Rocha and Nemisio Dominguez. The grant, which was authorized by the three-term alcalde (mayor of a Spanish town) of Los Angeles, Jose Antonio Carrillo, came with the stipulation that the tar pits remain public property. The proviso allowed registered residents of the surrounding pueblo to dip into the communal tar pits as they so pleased. Most used the asphalt to reinforce the roofs of their adobe dwellings. The deed to Rancho La Brea, which comprised of sections of what is now West Hollywood, present-day Hollywood's Wilshire's Miracle Mile, was formally confirmed by the governor of Alta California, Jose Maria de Echeandia, and was publicly acknowledged by Governor Juan Alvarado again in 1840.

In the spirit of due diligence, Rocha, along with his son Jose Jorge Rocha and Josefa de la Merced de Jordan, jointly lodged a claim with the Public Land Commission the following year. Much to their dismay, the case of Rancho La Brea remained in limbo for the next eight years, until it was repudiated by the court in 1860. Even so, the ranch owners persistently petitioned for the court to retry their case in a series of hearings, and they enlisted the aid of a former major, lawyer, and surveyor of the city of Los Angeles, Henry Hancock, to spearhead their efforts.

Hancock

As the *rancho* team battled it out at court, scientists across the state began to take steps to assuage the scientific interest that the La Brea Tar Pits had piqued. In 1853, shortly after New York-born geologist William Phipps Blake was appointed lead geologist of the Pacific

Railroad Survey of the Far West – chiefly to analyze, record his observations, and arrive at a theory on erosion in the geologic features of southern California – he paid a visit to the ranch. Blake became the first scientist to truly scrutinize the pits and its bitumen in depth, pinning his focus on a large pool of pitch measuring 30 feet in diameter. He made a marked reference to the bitumen's tendency to spill over and mix with pieces of sediment, which hardened into a thick layer, but maintained a soft consistency in the heart of the pit.

Blake

The pitch of the tar pits provided some of nature's best preservatives. Indeed, scrubbing the fossils clean with heated kerosene was a perilous and arduous process, but the black, viscous substance acted as an effective sealant that enveloped these bone bits and protected them against decay and degeneration, keeping them in near mint condition. This organic preservation method allowed the specimen to retain the subtlest and most delicate markings and details, such as the minuscule notches on the tooth of a carnivore, as well as imprints of networks of nerves and blood vessels. Even the full antennae, wings, and limbs of thumb-sized insects were occasionally discovered intact, and some blowfly pupae and other insect eggs were still clinging to bone marrow fissures. Without the La Brea-brand tar, it would have been extremely difficult for paleontologists to envision and establish grounded theories about southern California in the Ice Age.

Of course, regardless of the tar's exceptional preservative properties, the act of assembling the bones to form a complete creature – not unlike a free-form, frame-less puzzle – was an exceedingly intricate and toilsome task. Bones were strewn about and often entangled with the remnants of other creatures, and it was a rare stroke of luck to find a corpse of a tiny insect loosely strung together in the same place. The bones of the Pleistocene beasts were also severely mutilated, ranging from cracked fragments to saw-edged, splintered bits, which made it all the more difficult for scientists to piece together a coherent and cohesive skeleton in full.

Many of the county scientists' discoveries during this period altered a number of generally accepted views within the community. Larisa DeSantis broke down one such revelation: "Isotopes from the bones previously suggested that the diets of saber-toothed cats and dire wolves overlapped completely, but the isotopes from their teeth give a very different picture. The cats, including saber-toothed cats, American lions, and cougars, hunted prey that preferred forests, while it was the dire wolves that seemed to specialize on open-country feeders like bison and horses. While there may have been some overlap in what the dominant predators fed on, cats and dogs largely hunted differently from one another."

Remains of Pleistocene plants also put the spotlight on the ecology of the Los Angeles Basin during the thaw of the Ice Age. As gathered by researchers from the Los Angeles County Museum of History, Science, and Art, the canyon redwood groves and sage scrubs endemic to the basin during the Last Glacial Period indicates a far moister, peninsula-like climate than previously thought. In the immediate decades that followed, lasting well into the late 1950s, scores of academics and scientific illustrators were employed to not only keep track of the ever-growing inventory, but also to produce monographs and composite sketches of the various new species of mammals, birds, and plants brought to light.

Over 4,000 specimens belonging to the dire wolf have been discovered in the pits thus far, making it the most recurrent of all the species uncovered within the ranch. Saber-toothed cats, of which there are 2,000 specimens, was ranked the second most common animal found in the tar pits, and coyote specimens, which approached 1,000, placed third. The oldest specimen in the database, an estimated 44,000 years in age, belonged to a dire wolf.

The most frequently discovered herbivores in the ranch was most likely the *Bison antiquus*, or the ancient bison, which were muscular creatures with an average shoulder height of seven and-a-half feet. This, in turn, suggests that Ice Age bison were, as dictated by nature, swamp animals, as opposed to their modern counterparts, who are classed as prairie animals.

More intriguing yet, a whopping 90% of the La Brea mammals and vertebrates trapped in the pitch were carnivores, meaning there were nine carnivores to every herbivore. This is a particularly headscratching tidbit considering that this is an inverse to the standard ratio. Based on two separate studies conducted in the mid-20th century, which examined the wolf-to-deer and lion-to-plant-eater populations in Ontario and Minnesota, as well as across Africa, herbivores, on average, outnumbered carnivores between 100-150:1. The discrepancy of the missing herbivores at La Brea, some experts believe, lends further credence to the tar entrapment theory. The plights of herbivores who found themselves immobilized by the glutinous asphalt were compounded by vicious and hungry carnivorous predators who became ensnarled in the sludge themselves, which potentially explained the excessive amount of carnivores in the pits.

The bones of ancient gray wolves, cougars, and coyotes, when juxtaposed with the herculean skeletons of mammoths, mastodons, and short-faced bears, suggested that they were once considered small and meek, almost docile creatures. These comparatively petite predators tracked down and feasted on smaller critters, and they often hid themselves behind trees and boulders to pick at the corpses left behind by larger predators. DeSantis described the significance of this finding: "The...exciting thing about this research is we can actually look at the consequences of this extinction. The animals around today that we think of as apex predators in North America – cougars and wolves – were measly during the Pleistocene. So when the big predators went extinct, as did the large prey, these smaller animals were able to take advantage of that extinction and become dominant apex predators."

Somewhat fittingly, it was Hancock himself who presented to paleontologist William Denton the fateful *Smilodon* canine that set these wildly fruitful excavations in motion. The La Brea Tar Pits, considered one of the largest and most richly diverse wellsprings of Pleistocene-era fossils in the world, has since yielded more than three million identifiable specimens altogether, 130,000 of which are *Smilodon* bones belonging to at least 2,000 individual saber-toothed tigers.

The interest in the legendary creature has yet to die down, assisted by countless depictions in literature and other mediums of pop culture. On September 25th, 1973, Assembly Bill No. 940, signed by California Governor Ronald Reagan, came into effect, and with that the *Smilodon californicus* was declared the official fossil for the state of California. The bill's passage was anything but smooth, as it had been contested by W. Craig Biddle, a member of the California State Senate and one of Reagan's political opponents, who actively campaigned for the trilobites (ancient slug and beetle hybrids, or more specifically, marine arachnomorph arthropods), the oldest fossils ever to be found in California. In the end, state authorities evidently opted for the more glamorous choice.

In recent history, a smattering of alleged witnesses have also been urging scientists to reevaluate the extinct status of the genus. Ever since the *Smilodon* entered the mainstream consciousness, a steady flow of supposed saber-toothed tiger sightings have surfaced, none of which were ever confirmed due to the stark lack of physical evidence left behind. These two cases that follow were no different, but they make for interesting stories nonetheless.

In 1966, a naturalist and author named Peter Mattheisen related a South American seaman's apparent encounter with a frightening, bizarre-looking feline. A passage from Mattheisen's book, *The Cloud Forest,* reads, "[Picquet (the seaman)] described a rare striped cat not quite so large as a jaguar and very timid, which is possessed of two very large protruding teeth: this animal, he said, occurs in the mountain jungles of Columbia and Ecuador, and he has glimpsed it once himself."

In 1975, Karl Shuker, author of *Mystery Cats of the World,* described another supposed *Smilodon* sighting in Paraguay. The account in question was conveyed to him by a local zoologist named Juan Acavar, who claimed to have happened upon what he firmly believed was the 160-pound corpse of a saber-toothed tiger that bore a striking set of 12-inch fangs. The fcline, Acavar continued, died not of natural causes, but was killed by what seemed to be a stray bullet that had lodged itself in the beast's skull. Precisely why Acavar chose to keep mum about such a mindblowing discovery is unknown. He chose instead to identify the feline as a "mutant jaguar" in his report, perhaps fearing ridicule from his peers. Others say he chose to do so to prevent the other locals from panicking.

Modern society's fascination with the *Smilodon* – even outside of the scientific realm – does not appear to be going extinct anytime soon. In May 2004, a 16,000-year-old *Smilodon* skull extracted from a residential construction site by the La Brea Tar Pits fetched a price of $223,250 at a Beverly Hills auction. The winning bid was made by Stuart Pivar, a private collector from New York. In May 2009, another nearly intact *Smilodon* skull, complete with canines just over 12 inches in length, sold for a whopping $334,600 after it had been exhumed from the Wilshire/Hauser Tar Pit.

These dizzying price tags have only continued to escalate. In September 2019, another skull recovered from the La Brea Tar Pits was put up for auction. Due to the skull's almost pristine conditions and massive size – the anterior edge of the premaxilla to the end of the occipital condyles measured 355.5 mm in length – the precious item was expected to reel in anywhere between $700,000-$1,000,000.

Regardless of one's personal stance on the ownership of animal skulls, or any other faunal trophy or collectible for that matter, it is impossible to deny that the still-growing price tags for *Smilodon* remnants only further deepens the everlasting mystique of these saber-toothed beasts. The auctions are just one more piece of evidence demonstrating the fanged feline's unique and extraordinary legacy.

Online Resources

<u>Other books about ancient history by Charles River Editors</u>

<u>Other books about saber-toothed tigers on Amazon</u>

Bibliography

Amelar, S. (2019, August 30). Three Proposals for Transforming the La Brea Tar Pits. Retrieved January 30, 2020, from https://www.architecturalrecord.com/articles/14251-three-proposals-for-transforming-the-la-brea-tar-pits

Anton, M. (2013). *Sabertooth*. Indiana University Press.

Austin, O. L. (Ed.). (1987, January 30). The sabercat Smilodon gracilis from Florida and a discussion of its relationships (Mammalia, Felidae, Smilodontini). Retrieved January 30, 2020, from https://ufdc.ufl.edu/UF00095816/00001/10j

Barras, C. (2013, July 25). Zoologger: The pint-sized sabre-toothed opossum. Retrieved January 30, 2020, from https://www.newscientist.com/article/dn23933-zoologger-the-pint-sized-sabre-toothed-opossum/

Black, R. (2012, November 9). The Top 10 Greatest Survivors of Evolution. Retrieved January 30, 2020, from https://www.smithsonianmag.com/science-nature/the-top-10-greatest-survivors-of-evolution-118143319/

Bocherens, H., Cotte, M., & Bonini, R. (2015, August 4). Paleobiology of sabretooth cat Smilodon populator in the Pampean Region (Buenos Aires Province, Argentina) around the Last Glacial Maximum: Insights from carbon and nitrogen stable isotopes in bone collagen. Retrieved January 30, 2020, from https://www.academia.edu/22413053/Paleobiology_of_sa bretooth_cat_Smilodon_populator_in_the_Pampean_Regi on_Buenos_Aires_Province_Argentina_around_the_Last_ Glacial_Maximum_Insights_from_carbon_and_nitrogen_ stable_isotopes_in_bone_collagen

Bocherens, H. (2016, March 21). Saber-toothed cats hunted on the South American plains. Retrieved January 30, 2020, from https://www.academia.edu/23548787/Saber-toothed_cats_hunted_on_the_South_American_plains

Briggs, H. (2015, December 2). Did our ancient ancestors 'kill the cat'? Retrieved January 30, 2020, from https://www.bbc.com/news/science-environment-34944560

Castro, J. (2015, January 28). 1st Americans Used Spear-Throwers to Hunt Large Animals. Retrieved January 30, 2020, from https://www.livescience.com/49603-paleo-indian-spear-thrower-evidence.html

Choi, C. Q. (2012, December 27). Starvation Didn't Wipe Out Sabertooth Cats. Retrieved January 30, 2020, from https://www.livescience.com/25848-starvation-extinction-sabertooth-cats.html

Christiansen, P. (2006, July 14). Sabertooth characters in the clouded leopard (Neofelis nebulosa Griffiths 1821). Retrieved January 30, 2020, from https://onlinelibrary.wiley.com/doi/abs/10.1002/jmor.10468

Christiansen, P., & Harris, J. M. (2012, October 26). Variation in Craniomandibular Morphology and Sexual Dimorphism in Pantherines and the Sabercat Smilodon fatalis. Retrieved January 30, 2020, from https://journals.plos.org/plosone/article?id=10.1371/journal.pone.0048352

Clason, D. (2018, March 1). Hearing in the animal kingdom. Retrieved January 30, 2020, from https://www.healthyhearing.com/report/52843-Hearing-in-the-animal-kingdom

Cohen, J. (2018, August 22). Powerful Arms Saved Saber-Toothed Killers' Fearsome Fangs, Study Shows. Retrieved January 30, 2020, from https://www.history.com/news/powerful-arms-saved-saber-toothed-killers-fearsome-fangs-study-shows

Coleman, L., & Clark, J. (2013). *Cryptozoology A To Z: The Encyclopedia Of Loch Monsters Sasquatch Chupacabras And Other Authentic M.* Simon and Schuster.

Croft, D. A. (2016). *Horned Armadillos and Rafting Monkeys: The Fascinating Fossil Mammals of South America.* Indiana University Press.

Dell'amore, C. (2013, July 3). Sabertooths Had Weak Bites, Used Neck Muscles to Kill. Retrieved January 30, 2020, from https://www.nationalgeographic.com/news/2013/7/130702-sabertooth-cat-bite-prehistoric-science-animals/

Editors, A. W. (2018, November 14). Smilodon Facts For Kids & Adults: Discover One Of The World's Best-Known Prehistoric Animals. Retrieved January 30, 2020, from https://www.activewild.com/smilodon/

Editors, B. U. (1998). Introduction to the Gorgonopsia. Retrieved January 30, 2020, from https://ucmp.berkeley.edu/synapsids/gorgonopsia.html

Editors, B. U. (2011). What Is a Sabertooth? Retrieved January 30, 2020, from https://ucmp.berkeley.edu/mammal/carnivora/sabretooth.html

Editors, C. (2018, June 6). The Descendant Of The Saber-toothed Tiger May Disappoint You. Retrieved January 30, 2020, from https://www.cracked.com/article_25651_the-descendant-saber-toothed-tiger-may-disappoint-you.html

Editors, D. U. (2009, November 6). Male Sabertoothed Cats Were Pussycats Compared To Macho Lions. Retrieved January 30, 2020, from https://www.sciencedaily.com/releases/2009/11/091105121050.htm

Editors, D. A. (2017). The saber-toothed tiger (Smilodon). Retrieved January 30, 2020, from https://dinoanimals.com/animals/the-saber-toothed-tiger-smilodon/

Editors, E. I. (2013, July 30). Sabertooths Still Roam South America. Retrieved January 30, 2020, from https://evolution-institute.org/sabertooths-still-roam-south-america/

Editors, E. B. (2018, February 8). Miocene Epoch. Retrieved January 30, 2020, from https://www.britannica.com/science/Miocene-Epoch

Editors, F. E. (2019). California State Fossil - Saber-Tooth Tiger (Smilodon californicus). Retrieved January 30, 2020, from https://www.fossilera.com/pages/california-state-fossil-saber-tooth-tiger-smilodon-californicus

Editors, I. C. (2013). ANCIENT DNA CONNECTS SABER-TOOTHED TIGERS AND HOUSE CATS. Retrieved January 30, 2020, from https://www.inverse.com/article/37532-saber-toothed-tigers-cats-smilodon-homothereum

Editors, I. F. (2018). Humans Fought Saber-Toothed Cats In Europe. Retrieved January 30, 2020, from https://www.iflscience.com/plants-and-animals/humans-fought-saber-toothed-cats-europe/

Editors, L. T. (2004, May 3). Private Collector Buys Saber-Toothed Tiger Skull for $223,000. Retrieved January 30, 2020, from https://www.latimes.com/archives/la-xpm-2004-may-03-me-saber3-story.html

Editors, L. A. (2019, September 23). Rare saber-tooth cat skull fossil could make $1M at auction. Retrieved January

30, 2020, from https://www.liveauctioneers.com/news/top-news/naturalhistory/rare-fossil-to-lead-heritage-auctions-nature-science-sale/

Editors, N. G. (2013, April 2). Tracing the Roots of Smilodon. Retrieved January 30, 2020, from https://www.nationalgeographic.com/science/phenomena/2013/04/02/tracing-the-roots-of-smilodon/

Editors, N. G. (2013, November 11). A Living Sabertooth. Retrieved January 30, 2020, from https://www.nationalgeographic.com/science/phenomena/2013/11/11/a-living-sabertooth/

Editors, N. G. (2015, December 23). Did Sabercats Have Spotted and Striped Coats? Retrieved January 30, 2020, from https://www.nationalgeographic.com/science/phenomena/2015/12/23/did-sabercats-have-spotted-and-striped-coats/

Editors, P. B. (2001). Miocene Epoch (24-5.3 mya). Retrieved January 30, 2020, from https://www.pbs.org/wgbh/evolution/change/deeptime/miocene.html

Editors, P. W. (2011). Megantereon. Retrieved January 30, 2020, from http://www.prehistoric-wildlife.com/species/m/megantereon.html

Editors, P. W. (2012). Smilodon. Retrieved January 30, 2020, from http://www.prehistoric-wildlife.com/species/s/smilodon.html

Editors, P. H. (2012). SABER TOOTH CAT smilidon. Retrieved January 30, 2020, from http://www.prehistory.com/saberth.htm

Editors, P. F. (2013, April 7). Machairodus coloradensis. Retrieved January 30, 2020, from https://prehistoric-fauna.com/Machairodus-coloradensis

Editors, P. F. (2018, August 12). Smilodon gracilis. Retrieved January 30, 2020, from https://prehistoric-fauna.com/Smilodon-gracilis

Editors, R. G. (2015, March). Lateral view of the skulls of adult specimens of Monodelphis iheringi (A) and M. Retrieved January 30, 2020, from https://www.researchgate.net/figure/Lateral-view-of-the-skulls-of-adult-specimens-of-Monodelphis-iheringi-A-and-M_fig5_276071052

Editors, S. T. (2016). Saber Tooth Tiger Facts – Top 20 Most Amazing Facts. Retrieved January 30, 2020, from https://sabertoothtiger.org/saber-tooth-tiger-facts/

Editors, T. M. (1973, August 6). Science: Tiger in the Bank. Retrieved January 30, 2020, from

http://content.time.com/time/magazine/article/0,9171,904
005,00.html

Editors, T. T. (2011, December). CLOUDED
LEOPARD : A 'SABER-TOOTH' CAT. Retrieved
January 30, 2020, from http://tigertribe.net/clouded-
leopard-a-saber-tooth-cat/

Editors, T. I. (2013, December 17). Clouded Leopards:
Modern Semi-Sabertooth Cats. Retrieved January 30,
2020, from
https://tremendouslyimpressive.wordpress.com/2013/12/1
7/clouded-leopards-modern-sabertooth-cats/

Editors, U. T. (2014, April 1). Humans and saber-toothed
tiger met in Germany 300,000 years ago. Retrieved
January 30, 2020, from
https://www.sciencedaily.com/releases/2014/04/14040111
2022.htm

Editors, W. (2020, January 10). Smilodon. Retrieved
January 30, 2020, from
https://en.wikipedia.org/wiki/Smilodon

Editors, W. (2020, January 25). Felidae. Retrieved
January 30, 2020, from
https://en.wikipedia.org/wiki/Felidae

Editors, W. (2020, January 26). Gorgonopsia. Retrieved January 30, 2020, from https://en.wikipedia.org/wiki/Gorgonopsia

Editors, Y. J. (2019, May 9). Relatives of the Sabre Tooth. Retrieved January 30, 2020, from https://youngjournalistacademy.com/relatives-of-the-sabre-tooth/

Fleisher, N. (2009). Nearly Intact Saber-Tooth Skull Found Near La Brea Tar Pits At Heritage Auctions. Retrieved January 30, 2020, from https://www.ha.com/information/sabertooth.s

Gelbart, M. (2011, July 8). Two New Studies of Sabertooth (Smilodon fatalis) Anatomy. Retrieved January 30, 2020, from https://markgelbart.wordpress.com/2011/07/08/two-new-studies-of-sabertooth-smilodon-fatalis-anatomy/

Hecht, J. (2017, April 10). Sabre-toothed tigers in ice-age Los Angeles had bad back trouble. Retrieved January 30, 2020, from https://www.newscientist.com/article/2127141-sabre-toothed-tigers-in-ice-age-los-angeles-had-bad-back-trouble/

Hernandez, D. (2019, May 31). Saber-Toothed Cats Were Even More Vicious Than We Thought. Retrieved

January 30, 2020, from
https://www.popularmechanics.com/science/a27677964/s
aber-toothed-cat-skull/

Hilton, R. P., & Medeiros, J. (2018). Smilodon.
Retrieved January 30, 2020, from
https://www.sierracollege.edu/ejournals/jscnhm/v6n2/smil
odon.html

Holloway, A. (2014, June 5). New study blames humans
for megafauna extinction. Retrieved January 30, 2020,
from https://www.ancient-origins.net/news-evolution-
human-origins/new-study-blames-humans-megafauna-
extinction-001724

Hulbert, R. C. (2013, April 23). Smilodon fatalis.
Retrieved January 30, 2020, from
https://www.floridamuseum.ufl.edu/florida-vertebrate-
fossils/species/smilodon-fatalis

Katz, B. (2017, October 23). Saber-toothed Cats May
Have Co-Existed With Modern Humans. Retrieved
January 30, 2020, from
https://www.smithsonianmag.com/smart-news/saber-
toothed-cats-may-have-co-existed-modern-humans-
180965349/

MacElroy, A. (2013). Smilodon. Retrieved January 30,
2020, from

http://academic.emporia.edu/aberjame/student/mcelroy1/s milodon.htm

Mancini, M. (2015, August 23). 10 Fun Facts About Saber-Toothed Cats. Retrieved January 30, 2020, from https://www.mentalfloss.com/article/67220/10-fun-facts-about-saber-toothed-cats

Meachen, J. A., O'Keefe, F. R., & Sadleir, R. W. (2014, February 21). Evolution in the sabre-tooth cat, Smilodon fatalis, in response to Pleistocene climate change. Retrieved January 30, 2020, from https://onlinelibrary.wiley.com/doi/full/10.1111/jeb.12340

Minotti, M. (2016). Evidence of interaction of Pre-Clovis man with Smilodon fatalis. Retrieved January 30, 2020, from https://www.academia.edu/16626521/Evidence_of_intera ction_of_Pre-Clovis_man_with_Smilodon_fatalis

Moon, P. (2015). The man who faced the saber-toothed cat - Peter Wilhelm Lund's Forgotten Encounters with the Brazilian deep past and the colonial present. Retrieved January 30, 2020, from https://www.academia.edu/15632969/The_man_who_face d_the_saber-toothed_cat_-_Peter_Wilhelm_Lunds_Forgotten_Encounters_with_the_ Brazilian_deep_past_and_the_colonial_present

Moseman, A. (2010, July 7). The Saber-Toothed Cat's True Secret: Its Super-Strong Arms. Retrieved January 30, 2020, from https://www.discovermagazine.com/planet-earth/the-saber-toothed-cats-true-secret-its-super-strong-arms

Pappas, S. (2014, June 3). Humans Blamed for Extinction of Mammoths, Mastodons & Giant Sloths. Retrieved January 30, 2020, from https://www.livescience.com/46081-humans-megafauna-extinction.html

Pickrell, J. (2018, October 20). Saber-Toothed Cats May Have Roared Like Lions. Retrieved January 30, 2020, from https://www.scientificamerican.com/article/saber-toothed-cats-may-have-roared-like-lions/

Pickrell, J. (2019, March 24). Saber-toothed cats were fierce and family-oriented. Retrieved January 30, 2020, from https://www.sciencenews.org/article/saber-toothed-cats-smilodon

Polly, P. D. (1994, April 30). The Oligocene Epoch. Retrieved January 30, 2020, from http://ucmp-dev.berkeley.edu/tertiary/oligocene.php

Polly, P. D. (2017). SABER-TOOTHED CATS. Retrieved January 30, 2020, from https://igws.indiana.edu/FossilsAndTime/Sabertooth

Prieto, A., & Labarca, R. (2010). New evidence of the sabertooth cat Smilodon (Carnivora: Machairodontinae) in the late Pleistocene of southern Chilean Patagonia. Retrieved January 30, 2020, from https://scielo.conicyt.cl/scielo.php?script=sci_arttext&pid=S0716-078X2010000200010&lng=en&nrm=iso&tlng=en

Robins, B. (2018). THE REASON SABER-TOOTHED TIGERS WENT EXTINCT. Retrieved January 30, 2020, from https://www.grunge.com/168872/the-reason-saber-toothed-tigers-went-extinct/

Sailer, S. (2018, January 11). How Did Indians Exterminate Saber-Toothed Tigers? Retrieved January 30, 2020, from https://www.unz.com/isteve/how-did-indians-exterminate-saber-toothed-tigers/

Smith, R. (2009, November 5). SABERTOOTHED MALES WERE PUSSYCATS. Retrieved January 30, 2020, from https://today.duke.edu/2009/11/sabertooth.html

Solly, M. (2019, August 6). Fossils Reveal Why Coyotes Outlived Saber-Toothed Cats. Retrieved January 30, 2020, from https://www.smithsonianmag.com/smart-news/fossils-reveal-why-coyotes-outlived-saber-toothed-cats-180972826/

Strauss, B. (2019, July 3). Top 10 Saber-Toothed Tiger Facts. Retrieved January 30, 2020, from https://www.thoughtco.com/facts-about-the-saber-tooth-tiger-1093337

Stutsman, J. (2018, April 19). Why Did the Saber Tooth Tiger Go Extinct? Retrieved January 30, 2020, from https://sciencing.com/did-tooth-tiger-go-extinct-6113344.html

Switek, B. (2016, November 2). The Making of the Cat. Retrieved January 30, 2020, from https://www.pbs.org/wnet/nature/blog/the-making-of-a-cat/

Switek, B. (2017, April 3). Drawing Out a Sabercat's Smile. Retrieved January 30, 2020, from https://blogs.scientificamerican.com/laelaps/drawing-out-a-sabercats-smile/

Tabatabaie, C. (2017, May 31). What you need to know about smilodon, the real Nashville Predator. Retrieved January 30, 2020, from https://positivepeerpressure.blog/what-you-need-to-know-about-smilodon-the-real-nashville-predator-b7c982d13c47

Vocelle, L. (2012, July 31). WHO OR WHAT IS PSEUDAELURUS? Retrieved January 30, 2020, from https://www.thegreatcat.org/who-or-what-is-pseudaelurus/

Wallace, S. C., & Hulbert, R. C. (2013). A New Machairodont from the Palmetto Fauna (Early Pliocene) of Florida, with Comments on the Origin of the Smilodontini (Mammalia, Carnivora, Felidae). Retrieved January 30, 2020, from https://www.ncbi.nlm.nih.gov/pmc/articles/PMC3596359/

Whitfield, T. (2016, June 17). Reason behind sabre toothed tiger ice age extinction revealed. Retrieved January 30, 2020, from https://www.mirror.co.uk/news/world-news/reason-behind-sabre-toothed-tiger-8220741

Williams, A. (2015, November 4). Did Neanderthals and sabre-toothed wage battles? Fossil remains reveal the predators lived side-by-side with our ancestors. Retrieved January 30, 2020, from https://www.dailymail.co.uk/sciencetech/article-3303901/Did-Neanderthals-sabre-toothed-wage-battles-Fossil-remains-reveal-predators-lived-ancestors.html

Wilson, T. V. (2009). How Saber-tooth Cats Worked. Retrieved January 30, 2020, from https://science.howstuffworks.com/environmental/earth/geology/saber-tooth-cat4.htm

Free Books by Charles River Editors

We have brand new titles available for free most days of the week. To see which of our titles are currently free, click on this link.

Discounted Books by Charles River Editors

We have titles at a discount price of just 99 cents everyday. To see which of our titles are currently 99 cents, click on this link.